Alice's Wonderland

Alice's Wonderland

A Visual Journey through Lewis Carroll's Mad, Mad World

Catherine Nichols

Race Point
PUBLISHING

Acknowledgments

The author would like to thank Joan Kane Nichols and Karl Best for their thoughtful comments and unfailing support throughout the writing process.

Race Point Publishing
A division of Quarto Publishing Group USA Inc.
276 Fifth Avenue, Suite 205
New York, NY 10001

RACE POINT and the distinctive Race Point Publishing logo
are trademarks of Quarto Publishing Group USA Inc.

Author: Catherine Nichols
Interior Design: Jacqui Caulton
Cover Design: Heidi North

Please see page 201 for the photography and illustration credits

ISBN: 978-1-937994-97-6

Library of Congress Cataloging-in-Publication data is available

Printed in China

2 4 6 8 10 9 7 5 3

www.racepointpub.com

Contents

Foreword

by Mark Burstein

This foreword is not meant to introduce you to the Rev. Charles Lutwidge Dodgson; his nom de plume, Lewis Carroll; or the Alice books. In the first place, they are so pervasive throughout our culture that this "interminable fairy-tale," as Carroll called it in his diary, is nearly unavoidable. In the second place, Catherine Nichols has done a superb job in filling in the details in this wonderfully colorful compendium, which you are presumably about to read.

Children's literature can be divided into B.C. and A.D. (Before Carroll and After Dodgson), as his writings shed the pious morality and morbidity of earlier works for young juveniles and suddenly burst forth with the liberating light of imagination, rebelling against the conventions of the times with a topsy-turvy, wildly humorous, irreverent perspective. A book for children without lessons or cautionary lectures, filled with wordplay and paradox, and featuring a self-possessed heroine who questions all adult authority was not only quite a departure for children's books, but can be seen as a serious precursor of modern literature.

This present volume, *Alice's Wonderland*, is coming out just prior to the "sesquicenTenniel" (150th) year of the publication of *Alice's Adventures in Wonderland* in the late fall of 1865. (A white-vellum-bound copy was handed to the author's "infant patron" on the fourth of July of that year to commemorate the date on which he first told her and her sisters the tale as they rode up the Isis River, as the Thames is called at that point, three years earlier.) There will be celebrations all over the world; our organization, the Lewis Carroll Society of North America, is planning a glorious fête centered in New York in the fall of 2015, to be called Alice150.

Countless books have been written over the years celebrating these paradigm-shifting volumes, which are the most quoted novels in the English-speaking world and among the most widely illustrated, most translated, and, particularly since Martin Gardner's groundbreaking *Annotated Alice* (Clarkson Potter, 1960), most analyzed. My own modest collection has over three hundred different published book illustrators, and a scholarly book—*Alice in a World of Wonderlands* (Oak Knoll, 2015)—our Society is involved in publishing discusses translations into 140 languages (though some might argue that some of those are dialects). One of the factors that makes this present book special is Nichols's embracing of the Carrollian visions of those outside of published books: the filmmakers; set designers of stage, musicals, ballet, and opera; comic book, album art, fashion, advertising, and game creators; artists who publish on the Web; app designers; and the like.

When one begins to attempt to count (or collect) the various pastiches, "sequels," biographies, bibliographies, cookbooks, graphic novels, comics and manga, academic studies, annotations, speculations, compendia, collected works, books on Carroll's puzzles, logic, or photography, and other related books, the mind reels. Carroll himself, if one counts his pamphlets, was responsible for more than three hundred publications under his own name or pseudonym. Not to mention the sixty thousand or so letters he wrote.

It is impossible to estimate the number of copies of this book that have delighted children (and adults!) all over the globe over the last century and a half, though it is surely in the upper tens if not hundreds of millions.

Two of the reasons it is so widely illustrated are that Carroll included very few descriptions of Alice's appearance, and that he worked very closely with, one could say art directed, John Tenniel. An interesting anomaly is that in all the *Wonderland* merchandise Carroll ever authorized, which includes *The Nursery Alice* (1890; see page 6), which was colored by Tenniel and featured a cover by E. Gertrude Thomson; the Wonderland Postage-stamp Case (1889); and the De La Rue *Alice in Wonderland* card game (1894; see page 158), she is depicted wearing a *corn yellow* frock, though the apron is trimmed with blue and sports a large blue bow. Early printed editions also had her in a range of colors, but somehow, particularly after the 1951 Disney film, she has been associated almost exclusively with a blue dress.

As this book is intended to represent the better class of illustrations, painful choices had to be made. Inevitably, any Carrollian would have his or her particular favorites left out: for me, that would include illustrations by Charles Robinson (1907), Harry Rountree (1908), Nicole Claveloux (1974), Dušan Kállay (1981), Iassen Ghiuselev (2004), Anne Bachelier (2005), Jan Švankmajer (2006), Oleg Lipchenko (2007), Rébecca Dautremer (2010), and Xenia Lavrova (2013). Some amazing artists, such as Max Ernst (see page 28), Beatrix Potter, Edward Gorey, and the cartoonist Walt Kelly, made drawings, often unpublished, but not enough for a fully illustrated volume. The most comprehensive collection can be found in *Illustrating Alice* (Artists' Choice, 2013). One enterprising

gentleman, Michael Schneider, is currently attempting to tell the story *entirely without words*, by rounding up hundreds of artists, each of whom gets one sentence to depict in any style he or she wishes.

In my humble opinion, there has never been a truly satisfactory adaptation of the books in film or television; the closest for me is the Jonathan Miller teleplay (see page 81) with a cast that rivals that of the 1933 Paramount production (aside from those mentioned, one finds Alan Bennett, Michael Redgrave, Malcolm Muggeridge, and even Eric Idle). Speculation as to why there has never been a good cinematic adaptation revolve around the story being anecdotal, not developmental— that is, it's a series of vignettes rather than a narrative arc; that it has the standard translation problems, only magnified—i.e., if one only uses Carroll's dialogue, it can be overly familiar, but if it varies too much from it, it's akin to rewriting Shakespeare; and that for various Hollywood-en reasons it never got the full treatment that, say, *The Wonderful Wizard of Oz*, received. (As Nichols notes, Oz is very much a lesser light; while Alice has dozens of witty quotes and remarks that are an omnipresent part of our culture, there is not a single line from the Oz books that is familiar: they all come from the film.)

Alice's Wonderland is a superb introduction for those who wish to tumble down the rabbit-hole a bit deeper into the Carrollian universe, and is equally full of nuggets of interest for those of us who have been immersed in it for some time.

Mark Burstein
President
The Lewis Carroll Society of North America
www.LewisCarroll.org

Introduction

My first encounter with Lewis Carroll's plucky, pinafored heroine came in the form of a compliment. I was four years old and had been dining with my family at a favorite inn. The meal over, we were headed for the exit, when a woman stopped us. Bending down until she was eye level with me, she remarked how pretty my blue-and-white dress was, and that with my long blond hair held back with a wide band, I looked just like Alice in Wonderland. Clueless as I was of this mysterious Alice, something in the woman's voice told me it was an honor to be compared to her. It wasn't until much later, when I was in my teens, that I finally read *Alice's Adventures in Wonderland* from cover to cover in one sitting and realized how extraordinary a book it is and what an enduring character Alice is.

Carroll's achievement, I think, can partially be attributed to the immediacy and eccentricity of his story. From the moment the reader opens the book, he or she becomes Alice and experiences her travails. With her, the reader plunges down the rabbit hole, grows and shrinks, encounters strange creatures—a rabbit wearing a waistcoat, a hookah-smoking caterpillar, a disappearing cat—attends a mad tea party, and plays croquet with a queen. By the time the exhausted reader has stood trial and survived an attack by a pack of playing cards, like Alice, he or she will have confronted authority and triumphed over adversity. Closing the book, the reader is hopefully left with a feeling of catharsis and an appreciation for its author's originality and wit.

Since *Alice's Adventures in Wonderland* original publication in 1865 and *Through the Looking-Glass*

in 1871, the books have never been out of print. From the start, they captured the imaginations of readers everywhere and earned a place in the canon of Western literature. But more than just residing on dusty bookshelves, the books have wedged their way into the heart of popular culture. The books' characters have leapt off the page and found a home on the world's stages, movie screens, and television sets, and in galleries and shops. They are also the most widely quoted texts after Shakespeare and the Bible. So just what is it about Carroll's works that has caused this level of endurance and adoration? Why have they remained so popular even when other children's books from the Victorian era have long been forgotten?

The answer to all the above questions, perhaps, is that the books can be interpreted in infinite ways. Children can enjoy them at face value as adventurous stories; adults can delight in Carroll's ready wit and parodies of social conventions; and critics and academics can delve into the multiple psychological layers of meaning the text provides.

While researching this book, I visited Oxford, England, Lewis Carroll's home for thirty years and where he wrote both Alice tales. While strolling the city's cobblestone streets, I saw numerous examples of the books' influence and tributes to one of its most famous denizens. A flyer advertised a Mad Hatter's Tea Party at Christ Church; another told of an upcoming ballet performance in a neighboring town; a tea-and-coffee shop's window displayed promotional *Alice in Wonderland* teacups and mugs; a rare bookstore featured various illustrated first editions; and the Old Sheep Shop, a store that Carroll famously included in *Through the Looking-Glass* and that is now devoted to Alice merchandise, had its shelves crammed with Alice-related books, postcards, T-shirts, tote bags, Wonderland dolls, and more. Museum exhibits showcased Carroll's clever inventions and gadgets, as well as more Wonderland memorabilia. Perhaps most telling is the popular Alice in Wonderland cruise that winds upriver, following the route that Carroll took when he first told his tale to three spellbound children.

If you require further proof of the books' continuing relevance in today's culture, do an Internet search for "Alice" and "Wonderland" and see the number of searches that result. The day I tried, almost forty million hits came up. Not bad for a book about to celebrate its 150th anniversary.

The Alice adaptations I delve into here span the centuries. Almost immediately after *Alice's Adventures in Wonderland*'s publication, derivative works sprouted on the fertile ground he sowed. Carroll was alive to see the first stage production of his most famous work, an 1886 comedy titled *Alice in Wonderland: A Musical Dream Play*. He likewise might have played the first Alice-inspired card game (1882) or read any of the numerous literary imitations of his books, such as Anna Richardson's *A New Alice in the Old Wonderland* (1895).

In the twentieth century, new adaptations abounded. Alice made her first appearance on film in 1903 in a Hepworth Studio production that lasted all of twelve minutes. Since the early days of cinema, moviegoers have sat through many more Alice-based films, both live action and animated. And as the TV era dawned, producers for the small screen jumped on the Alice bandwagon, the first show making its appearance in 1937.

As the twenty-first century advances, interest in Lewis Carroll's two most famous works shows no sign of abating. The only change has been in technology. Instead of being able to buy just physical copies of the books, readers can now download the titles onto their PCs or tablets. They can purchase Alice-inspired apps, play video games that employ Alice as a weapon-collecting avatar, and watch movies about Wonderland on IMAX 3D screens.

As for the future? While we have no way of knowing what technological wizardry will develop, there is one thing we can count on: *Alice's Adventures in Wonderland* and *Through the Looking-Glass* will remain fixtures in our popular culture. And for that, this former Alice-in-Wonderland look-alike is supremely grateful.

—**Catherine Nichols**

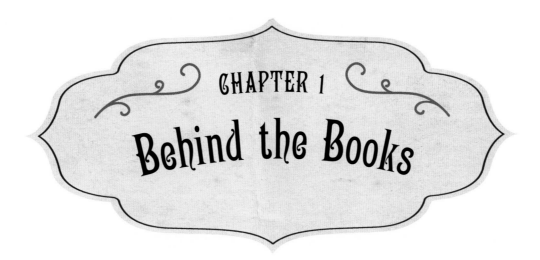

CHAPTER 1
Behind the Books

"Begin at the beginning," the King said gravely,
"and go on till you come to the end: then stop."

—Lewis Carroll, *Alice's Adventures in Wonderland*

In the summer of 1862, Lewis Carroll (a pseudonym for Charles Lutwidge Dodgson) was a thirty-year-old bachelor living at Christ Church in Oxford, England. A mathematics instructor, he was known throughout the college for his boring and uninspired lectures. But his students might have been surprised to see their stammering teacher when he was outside the classroom and in the company of his favorite audience—children.

As the third-oldest in a brood of eleven, Carroll was well versed in entertaining young minds. Born in 1832 to the Reverend Charles Dodgson and Frances Jane Lutwidge, the ever-resourceful older sibling put on puppet shows, performed magic tricks, and, of course, told endless stories to amuse his brothers and sisters in the old parsonage at Daresbury, Cheshire. So when he came to Christ Church—first as a student and later as an instructor—it was only natural that he sought out the same kind of family environment he had left behind. He found such a substitute family with the young children of the Dean of Christ Church, Henry George Liddell, and his wife Lorina. Carroll first made friends with Harry, the eldest child, in 1855, when the boy was nine. Before long he was introduced to Harry's sisters, Lorina, or Ina as she was known, Alice, and baby Edith. Carroll was immediately swept up into family life to the extent that Ina once remarked, "I don't know how we first knew Mr. Dodgson."

How Charles Dodgson Became Lewis Carroll

When twenty-four-year-old Charles Dodgson submitted his poem "Solitude" to the magazine *Train* in 1854, its editor, Edmund Yates, suggested that he use a pseudonym in order to separate his creative writings from his academic publications on mathematics. Carroll sent him four pseudonyms all based on variations of his name: Edgar Cuthwellis, Edgar U. C. Westhill, Louis Carroll, and Lewis Carroll. Yates selected the last and the rest is history.

An intensely private person with a "morbid dislike of publicity," Dodgson went out of his way to keep his two identities separate. He asked the librarian at Oxford University to remove the cross-references of his two names (a request denied) and returned mail addressed to Lewis Carroll to the sender, preparing a statement that read in part:

"Mr. Dodgson is so frequently addressed by strangers on the quite unauthorized assumption that he claims, or at any rate acknowledges the authorship of books not published under his own name, that he has found it necessary to print this, once for all, as answer to all such applications. He neither claims nor acknowledges any connection with any pseudonym, or with any book that is not published under his own name . . . . "

By the summer of 1862, Harry was away at boarding school, but that didn't stop Carroll from continuing to socialize with his younger sisters. He took them out on frequent excursions, usually with a friend or relative in tow. On July 4 of that year, Carroll, most likely dressed in white flannel trousers and a white straw hat, gathered his friend the Reverend Canon Robinson Duckworth and Lorina (age twelve), Alice (age ten), and Edith (age eight) for a boat trip along a stretch of the Thames that ran from Oxford to Godstow, where the group would stop to picnic.

They had gone on such boating adventures before, singing songs and playing games as they rowed, but this time was different. Alice, perhaps restless from the long day, asked Carroll for a story, and to amuse her he started one that featured her. This in itself wasn't unusual, for Carroll was famous for his entertaining stories. On this trip, though, Alice requested something new: she wanted her grown-up friend to write down his story for her.

The following day, as he journeyed from Oxford to London by train, Carroll jotted a rough outline of the story he had told the sisters, and added some other stories he had related on previous occasions.

The three Liddell sisters: Edith (left), Lorina (center), and Alice (right) in a photograph taken by Carroll around 1859.

But it wasn't until November of that year, with summer long past, that Carroll started writing the story in earnest. By March of the following year, he was ready to start on the illustrations, which he drew himself.

Original cover and pages of *Alice's Adventures under Ground*; the manuscript now resides at the British Museum in London.

In November 1864, the finished book, entitled *Alice's Adventures under Ground*, was presented to Alice. It is inscribed, "A Christmas Gift to a Dear Child, in Memory of a Summer Day." The green vellum-bound book, its title page designed with intertwined flowers, was handwritten by the author and included thirty-seven of his own illustrations.

Encouraged by friends to publish the story, Carroll got to work on another edition. He deleted the parts that directly referenced the Liddell sisters, expanded some chapters and added others, and created new characters—the Cheshire Cat and the members of the Mad Tea Party, for instance, make no appearance in the original manuscript. Carroll also revised some of the poems, most notably "The Mouse's Tail." And he came up with a new title. Concerned that *Alice's Adventures under Ground* might be misconstrued to be a book about mines, he renamed his creation *Alice's Adventures in Wonderland*.

Interpreting Alice

After Alice's tumble down the rabbit hole, she finds herself in an unfamiliar land with unfathomable rules. She shrinks, grows, and meets a bewildering cast of characters, all of whom seem to go out of their way to be disagreeable or contrary. She undergoes a series of trials and ultimately survives, intact, back in the loving arms of her sister. Many critics have interpreted Carroll's masterpiece, offering a multitude of theories, but it seems safe to say that the novel shows a young child navigating the complex world of adults and emerging both unscathed and wiser. No doubt that underlying message is what keeps *Alice's Adventures in Wonderland* fresh for young readers of today.

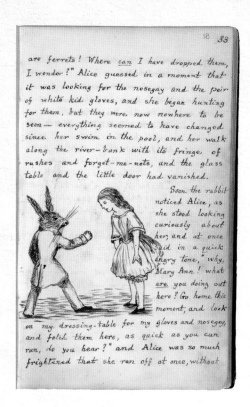

Carroll's illustrations of the White Rabbit addressing Alice as his servant Mary Ann (left) and of the guinea pigs and other animals assisting Bill, the Lizard (right).

With the manuscript completed to his satisfaction, Carroll turned his attention to finding an illustrator. Originally he wanted to use his own illustrations, but upon reflection, he realized he wasn't a draftsman; though, judging from his illustrations in *Alice's Adventures under Ground*, he wasn't without artistic talent.

Today it is inconceivable to imagine the Wonderland books without John Tenniel's illustrations, but in hiring Tenniel, Carroll made an unconventional choice and an expensive one—an illustrator of Tenniel's caliber did not come cheaply. At the time, Tenniel, a frequent contributor for the magazine *Punch*, was famous for his political cartoons.

Although Carroll ceded his position as illustrator, he still had very firm ideas about what the drawings should look like, and he made sure that Tenniel knew his desires. Carroll, a perfectionist with a reputation for being fussy, made more than his fair share of suggestions to the artist, but he was usually willing to concede to Tenniel's artistic expertise when differences arose. One area where they continued to disagree was over the use of a model. In a letter to his friend the artist E. Gertrude Thomson, Carroll complained:

"Mr. Tenniel is the only artist, who has drawn for me, who has resolutely refused to use a model, and declared he no more needed one than I should need a multiplication table to work a mathematical problem! I venture to think he was mistaken and that for want of a model, he drew several pictures of 'Alice' entirely out of proportion—head decidedly too large and feet decidedly too small."

On July 4, 1865, three years after Alice Liddell's request for a book about her, Macmillan and Company in London published two thousand copies of *Alice's Adventures in Wonderland*. Tenniel, however, was displeased with the quality of the printing and Carroll backed him up. The books were withdrawn from publication and Carroll—who, under his deal with the publisher, was responsible for the cost—paid the entire six hundred pounds for another printing. A new edition was published the following year.

"A glorious artistic treasure," "Amusingly written," and "Full of humor" were just a few of the rave reviews that *Alice's Adventures in Wonderland* received when it first came on the scene. Although the book was praised by almost every major reviewer, not everyone regarded Carroll's labor of love as an instant classic. A reviewer for the *Athenaeum* wrote on December 16, 1886: "We fancy that any child might be more puzzled than enchanted by this stiff, overwrought story."

The Boating Party

Carroll immortalized the original boating party in chapter two of *Alice's Adventures in Wonderland*: Alice finds herself in the predicament of swimming in a pool of her own tears, made when she was much larger. As she paddles, other animals fall in. "There was a Duck and a Dodo, a Lory and an Eaglet, and several other curious creatures." Carroll meant the birds to stand in for the people who accompanied him up the Thames on July 4, 1862. He included himself as well. Dodo is a play on Carroll's given last name, Dodgson, and in fact one of his nicknames was Dodo. The Duck was his friend the Reverend Robinson Duckworth. The Lory, a type of parrot, was Lorina, Alice's older sister, and the Eaglet was her younger sister, Edith.

The Dodo presents Alice with a thimble. In this illustration, legendary
artist John Tenniel gave the Dodo hands.

Carroll eventually shortened and simplified *Alice's Adventures in Wonderland* to make it accessible for younger children "from nought to five." Published in 1890 and titled *The Nursery Alice*, the book contained twenty of Tenniel's original illustrations, enlarged and colorized; E. Gertrude Thomson provided the new cover illustration.

Above: E. Gertrude Thomson's first-edition cover for *The Nursery Alice.*

With accolades flowing in, Carroll was pleased by his book's reception and his thoughts, therefore, turned to a sequel. In December 1867, he wrote to a friend: "Alice's visit to Looking-Glass House is getting on pretty well." However, two more years passed before he completed the book.

In *Alice's Adventures in Wonderland*, Carroll used a deck of playing cards as major players in his plot. He based his sequel, however, on the intricacies of chess. A lover of games and puzzles, Carroll re-created a real chess game in its pages, played on an immense chessboard with fields standing in for the squares. Alice is once again the protagonist, and through the course of her adventures, she encounters the various chess pieces in her quest to advance from pawn to queen.

In 1932, Alice, now known by her married name, Hargreaves, wrote that much of the book came from stories told before the famous boat ride on the Thames, "particularly the ones to do with chessmen, which are dated by the period when we were excitedly learning chess."

* * *

Carroll wanted Tenniel to illustrate his second book, but Tenniel turned him down, stating he was too busy with other projects. Carroll then approached other illustrators without success. Finally, after much persuading, Tenniel agreed to illustrate the new book, *Through the Looking-Glass and What Alice Found There*, but took his time producing the drawings. It wasn't until Christmas of 1871 that the book was published.

Tenniel's fifty illustrations were well worth the wait. As usual, Carroll and Tenniel tussled over the art. Carroll instructed the artist not to give Alice's dress "so much crinoline" and was adamant that the White Knight not have whiskers. Tenniel won the latter battle and another major one as well: He convinced Carroll to drop an entire chapter, "Wasp in a Wig," from the book. "Don't think me brutal," he wrote, "but I am bound to say that the 'wasp' character doesn't interest me in the least and I can't see my way to a picture."

Carroll had issues with another illustration meant to be the book's frontispiece: Tenniel's Jabberwock, "with eyes of flame," was so terrifying that Carroll worried that children would be scared out of their wits. Carroll sent copies of the drawing to thirty mothers, soliciting their opinions. The maternal panel backed him up and the fearsome Jabberwock was banished from the frontispiece.

Like *Alice's Adventures in Wonderland*, the sequel was a success with both the public and the critics. Carroll lived to see sales of more than 250,000 copies for the two books combined. In fact, since being published, neither book has ever gone out of print. They have been translated into more than 125 languages, including Hawaiian, Yiddish, and Esperanto.

Right: Tenniel's monstrous drawing of the Jabberwock has the body of a dragon, the head of a toothed fish, antennae, and talons. Alice recites a poem about the beast in the first chapter of *Through the Looking-Glass.*

The Real Alice

Unlike her fictional counterpart, who remains a child, forever locked in the pages of Wonderland, the real Alice grew up and put away childish things, like asking for stories from gentlemen friends. Born on May 4, 1852, Alice Pleasance Liddell, the inspiration for Carroll's timeless tales, became a rather conventional matron. Once linked in romance to Prince Leopold, Queen Victoria's youngest son, Alice married Reginald Hargreaves, a well-off man with whom she had three sons, two of whom died in World War I.

Carroll's ties with the Liddell family became strained around the time he was publishing *Alice's Adventures in Wonderland*. In June 1863, the author somehow managed to offend Alice Liddell's mother and was exiled from family gatherings. The cause for the rift is unknown, and the crucial pages from Carroll's diary were torn out after his death, so the mystery is unlikely to ever be solved. The consequence of the falling out, though, was that Carroll rarely saw Alice. He did stay in limited contact with her, sending her his books as they were published, as well as a wedding present.

In 1928, when she was in her late seventies, Alice sold the manuscript Carroll had given her. Sotheby's auctioned *Alice's Adventures under Ground* for 15,400 pounds, a tremendous amount of money for the time. An American dealer bought it, and the manuscript stayed across the pond until 1948, when it was bought and returned to England in appreciation of the country's war efforts. Today, *Alice's Adventures under Ground* resides inside the British Museum in London for all to see.

At the end of the handwritten manuscript of *Alice's Adventures under Ground,* Carroll drew Alice's portrait. Perhaps he wasn't satisfied with the results because he later pasted one of his own photographs of Alice over the drawing.

That same year, Alice agreed to an interview with the *New York Times* and recounted the boating trip that led to the creation of *Alice's Adventures in Wonderland:*

"The beginning of *Alice in Wonderland* was told to me one summer afternoon when the sun was so hot we landed in the meadows down the river, deserting the boat to take refuge in the only bit of shade to be found, which was under a newly made hayrick. Here from all three of us, my sisters and myself, came the old petition, 'Tell us a story,' and Mr. Dodgson began it."

According to Reverend Duckworth, the only other adult on the trip, *Alice's Adventures in Wonderland* was told while in the boat. "I rowed stroke and he [Carroll] rowed bow in the famous Long Voyage to Godstow, when the three Miss Liddells were our passengers, and the story was actually composed and spoken over my shoulder for the benefit of Alice

Liddell . . . ." Another interesting conundrum is that all the participants agree with Alice that the day was bright and hot; in fact, according to the weather report, it was cloudy and cool.

Although she had begged for the story, Alice gradually became weary of the attention it brought.

In a letter to her only surviving son, she wrote, "But oh my dear I am tired of being Alice in Wonderland. Does it sound ungrateful? It is. Only I do get so tired."

On November 15, 1934, at the age of eighty-two, Alice Pleasance Liddell Hargreaves died.

Lewis Carroll's contemporary, photographer Julia Margaret Cameron, took this photograph of Alice Liddell when she was twenty years old. Posed against lush foliage, Liddell is meant to represent Pomona, the Roman goddess of orchards and gardens.

Turning Children's Literature on Its Head

"Everything's got a moral, if only you can find it."
—Lewis Carroll, *Alice's Adventures in Wonderland*

Alice's Adventures in Wonderland proved to be a turning point in the world of children's literature, heralding a golden age that continued even through the arrival of A. A. Milne's Winnie-the-Pooh books in the 1920s. With his original book's publication, Lewis Carroll broke with tradition and established a fantasy world where anything could—and did—take place. Determined that his books not be burdened with dreary morals and cautionary tales, he concentrated on making them entertaining to read, cramming them with puns, puzzles, and riddles. Children, he suggested, learn best when their imaginations are allowed to run free rather than when their heads are stuffed with rules on how to behave.

As an example of Carroll's aversion to morals, Carroll sent a book titled *The Fountains of Youth* to Lilia MacDonald, daughter of the children's author George MacDonald, in 1867 and instructed her in a letter: "The book is intended for you to look at the outside, and then put it away in the bookcase: the inside is not meant to be read. The book has got a moral—so I need hardly say it is *not* by Lewis Carroll."

Carroll's books were in contrast to most of the books that Victorian children were reading. Religious publishers looked askew at fairy tales and fantasy, and produced grim, moralistic fare intended to instruct children on how to become upstanding citizens. Commercial publishers, while not as dour, thought it necessary to combine character building along with entertainment.

One book that broke this mold was Catherine Sinclair's *Holiday House*, published in 1839. The book's two protagonists, Harry and Laura, are presented as high-spirited and questioning, a far cry from the well-behaved, somewhat dull children in countless other books of the day. An immediate success, the tale was one of the first books to accept children as they really are, rather than how adults want them to be. Twenty years after its publication, it was still in print, and Carroll bought it as a Christmas present for the Liddell sisters in 1859.

Despite the publication of *Alice's Adventures in Wonderland*, the Victorian appetite for moralistic books did not dissipate overnight. In 1867, Hesba Stretton's novel *Jessica's First Prayer* was published to great acclaim. It tells the story of Jessica, a homeless girl with an alcoholic mother, who is befriended and helped by a religious man. The influential book began a fashion for tales about street urchins, homeless children who lived on city streets. *Jessica's First Prayer* was hugely popular, selling more than a million copies, leaving *Alice's Adventures in Wonderland* in the dust.

Another important children's book published just two years before *Alice's Adventures in Wonderland* was Reverend Charles Kingsley's *The Water-Babies*. Kingsley, a friend of Carroll's and one of the people who had urged him to turn *Alice's Adventures under Ground* into a proper book, wrote the fantasy of Tom, a young chimney sweep, who drowns and is transformed into a four-inch-tall water-baby. In his watery home, Tom is purified and given a moral education by fairies with names such as Mrs. Doasyouwouldbedoneby and Mrs. Bedonebyasyoudid. Although didactic, Kingsley's moral fable was also entertaining and extremely popular throughout the Victorian era.

This famous photograph, taken by Carroll in 1858, shows Alice Liddell dressed as a street urchin. The poet Alfred Lord Tennyson considered it the most beautiful photograph he'd ever seen.

The People Behind the Wonderland and Looking-Glass Characters

According to some interpreters, Carroll drew upon some of Victorian England's famous—and not-so-famous—figures when populating his cast of characters.

The White Rabbit

Notoriously late for his appointments, Dean Henry Liddell, the father of Alice and her siblings, is thought to be the inspiration for the ever-tardy White Rabbit.

The Hatter

Theophilus Carter was an eccentric cabinetmaker and furniture dealer well known around Oxford for being a bit odd. He dabbled in inventing, with one of his more famous creations being an "alarm clock bed" that woke slugabeds by tipping them onto the floor, which may explain the Hatter's obsession with time.

Carroll suggested to Tenniel that he draw the Hatter to resemble Carter, and it's likely that the illustrator did so—Carter frequently wore a top hat, just like the Hatter's.

The Dormouse

The sleepy dormouse that dozes in the teapot throughout the Mad Tea Party might have been based on a pet wombat kept by the poet and painter Dante Gabriel Rossetti, who often brought the creature to dinner, allowing it to sleep in a centerpiece on the dining-room table. Carroll knew Rossetti and his sister Christina, also a poet, and took photos of them and other members of their family.

THE DORMOUSE IN THE TEAPOT.

Conger-Eel

In Alice's pun-heavy exchange with the Mock Turtle about his education in *Alice's Adventures in Wonderland*, the turtle mentions that his "Drawling-master was an old conger-eel, that used to come once a week: he taught us Drawling, Stretching, and Fainting in Coils." The conger-eel is a reference to the great art critic John Ruskin, who instructed the Liddell sisters in drawing, sketching, and painting in oils. Carroll was good friends with Ruskin, even if the critic did discourage him from devoting too much time to sketching, telling Carroll he didn't have enough talent to make it worth his while.

The Sheep

In *Through the Looking-Glass*, Alice meets an old sheep, the proprietor of a shop filled with "all manner of curious things," who is busy knitting. When Alice Liddell was a child she used to frequent a candy shop owned by an old woman who was always knitting. Tenniel based his drawing on the actual shop, and it still exists today: a souvenir shop for all things Alice, it can be found at 83 Saint Aldgate Street in Oxford.

The Red Queen

Carroll once referred to the Red Queen ("one of the thorny kind") as "the concentrated essence of all governesses," with her endless morals and commands to "Look up, speak nicely, and don't twiddle your thumbs all the time." It is probable that he had the Liddell sisters' own governess, Mary Prickett, in mind when he penned this particular character. Nicknamed Pricks by her small charges, Prickett was once believed to be linked romantically to Carroll, although there appears to be no truth to the rumors.

The White Knight

When Carroll depicted the White Knight as having shaggy hair, a gentle face, and mild eyes, he was likely describing himself. There are other similarities between the knight and his creator: Both liked gadgets and both tried their hand at inventing. (Carroll's inventions included a case for postage stamps and a writing tablet that let the writer jot down notes in the dark.) The White Knight also treats the fictional Alice with genuine respect, unlike the other characters. He even offers Alice a heartfelt good-bye as she leaves him in her journey to become queen in the same way Carroll bids adieu to Alice Liddell as she becomes a young woman.

Charles Lutwidge Dodgson, the Man Behind the Books

"Who are *you*?" the Caterpillar asks Alice when she stumbles across him in Wonderland. The same question, when applied to Charles Lutwidge Dodgson (aka Lewis Carroll), would produce a range of responses, many of them contradictory.

A tall, thin man with longer hair than was the fashion, Dodgson had asymmetrical features and, according to Alice Liddell, carried himself upright, "as if he had swallowed a poker." His good friend E. Gertrude Thomson, an artist, described him as thus: "His head was small, and beautifully formed; the brow rather low, broad, white, and finely modeled. Dreamy grey eyes, a sensitive mouth, slightly compressed when in repose, but softening into the most beautiful smile when he spoke." He spoke with a stammer that he battled mightily to overcome.

The eccentric, persnickety don of Christ Church disliked cut flowers; had a horror of drafts; was obsessed with the number forty-two, peppering the number throughout his literary output; preferred girls over boys, once writing, "I am fond of children (except boys)"; dined on small portions of simple food and avoided luncheons since he had "no appetite for a meal at that time"; and enjoyed long walks of twenty-plus miles. He was also generous to a fault—with his time, money, and resources. He went out of his way to help people find work or advancement in their careers. He supplemented his cousin's widow's income and turned over the profits from the facsimile of *Alice's Adventure's under Ground* to hospitals and homes for sick children. When friends in need wrote to him for loans, on several occasions he replied, "I will not *lend*, but I will give you the 100 pounds you ask for."

Friends, relatives, and acquaintances had differing views of him. For instance, a playwright acquaintance described him as "a quiet, retiring, scholarlike person, full of interesting and pleasant conversation." Another friend remarked that Dodgson "was not a brilliant talker; he was too peculiar and paradoxical; and the topics on which he loved to dwell were such as would bore many persons." A niece conceded that "many . . . found him to be difficult, exacting, and uncompromising in business matters and in college life."

Portrait of Charles Lutwidge Dodgson (Lewis Carroll).

Children, however, adored him. His lodgings at Christ Church were crowded with all sorts of toys and games for their amusement, including a bear that could open and close its mouth. And in spite of his declaration that he didn't care for boys, he made friends with a number of them, including the Liddell sisters' older brother, Harry. Bert Coote, a child actor he befriended, said of Dodgson, ". . . he was one of us, and never a grown-up pretending to be a child in order to preach at us, or otherwise instruct us."

Dodgson was also an accomplished photographer, much admired for the elaborately staged pictures he took. Photography was in its early years when he began his hobby in 1856. Throughout the decades he perfected his skills and was hailed for the technical mastery of his images as well as for his keen eye. He prevailed upon many of his friends and acquaintances to sit for him and secured photographs of some of England's leading artistic figures, such as the poets Alfred Lord Tennyson and Dante Gabriel Rossetti.

Today, Dodgson is remembered for his photographs of nude little girls, most of which have been destroyed. Before a session in front of the camera, Dodgson was scrupulous in obtaining parental permission and ascertaining that the children were comfortable being photographed as a "daughter of Eve." While today taking such photographs would land the photographer in court, in England at this time, sketches and drawings of naked children were far from unusual; Victorians saw childhood as a time of innocence, free from sexuality.

It was later, in the Freudian era, that people began to reevaluate Dodgson's fascination with naked prepubescent girls. Many critics were quick to label him a pedophile. At the very least, he was assumed to be suppressing unhealthy desires. Recently, however, a reassessment of Dodgson has taken hold. Letters suggest that contrary to the long-held belief that he had no interest in women, Dodgson indeed had an eye for the ladies. The son of one of Dodgson's friends went so far as to dub him "a greying satyr in sheep's clothing."

Scholars continue to debate Dodgson's sexuality, and since Dodgson was among the most private of men who rarely wrote about his feelings, it is likely that the true nature of his relationships with young girls and women will never be fully understood.

At the age of sixty-four, in a letter to his sister, Dodgson wrote of death, ". . . more and more one realizes that it is an experience that each of *us* has to face, before long. The fact is getting *less* dreamlike to me, now: and I sometimes think what a grand thing it will be to be able to say to oneself 'Death is *over*, now: there is not *that* experience to be faced, again!'" Dodgson faced that particular experience on January 14, 1898, less than two weeks before his sixty-sixth birthday, dying suddenly from a bronchial infection. He was buried in Mount Cemetery in Guildford, Surrey, on a gray winter day.

In 1982, a stone memorial was placed and dedicated to him at Westminster Abbey. In the center, an inscription from one of his poems reads, "Is all our Life, then, but a dream?"

CHAPTER 2
Alice's Illustrators

"What is the use of a book," thought Alice,
"without pictures or conversations?"

—**Lewis Carroll**, *Alice's Adventures in Wonderland*

Surprisingly, Lewis Carroll gives very few descriptions in his books of what Wonderland and its inhabitants look like. As he himself advises in Chapter IX of *Alice in Wonderland*, "If you don't know what a Gryphon is, look at the picture." This lack of authorial direction gave his many illustrators free rein to imagine Wonderland to their liking. John Tenniel, the books' first illustrator, set a standard of such excellence that many readers can imagine Wonderland no other way. While Tenniel's is the unparalleled version, many other illustrators have left notable impressions as well. Some, such as Willy Pogany in the late 1920s, sought to modernize Alice. Arthur Rackham saw Wonderland as a mysterious, dangerous place filled with threatening characters. In our own time, Helen Oxenbury gave Alice back to children, creating an innocent Wonderland free from strife. Whatever the illustrator's vision, the many and diverse depictions serve to enhance our appreciation for Carroll's curious world.

John Tenniel (1820–1914)

Every artist who has illustrated *Alice in Wonderland* or *Through the Looking-Glass* owes an immense debt to John Tenniel.

An 1878 caricature of Tenniel by *Vanity Fair* portrait artist Leslie Ward.

Born in London in 1820, Tenniel was a skilled artist from an early age (although his "youthful aspiration" was to be a clown in a circus). He studied at the Royal Academy Schools before dropping out to follow his own independent study of art. In 1848, his black-and-white illustrations for an edition of *Aesop's Fables* intrigued the editor of *Punch*, a popular weekly satirical magazine. Before long, Tenniel was working for the magazine, an association that would last for nearly half a century. Throughout his long career he produced more than two thousand political cartoons for *Punch*. In 1893, Queen Victoria knighted Tenniel in recognition of his work at *Punch*; he was the first illustrator to be so honored.

Carroll, an enthusiastic reader of *Punch*, admired Tenniel's political cartoons, and even kept a collection of ones he had especially enjoyed and had clipped from the magazine's pages. So when Carroll was looking for an artist to illustrate *Alice in Wonderland*, it was natural that he should think of him.

Once Tenniel received the manuscript for *Alice in Wonderland*, he had quite a task in front of him. Carroll often was vague when it came to how a certain character looked. Even Alice, the story's protagonist, isn't described at length. In Chapter II, Alice says she's sure she's not Ada "for her hair goes in such long ringlets, and mine doesn't go in ringlets at all." And except for a reference from the Hatter that "her hair wants cutting"— from which can be inferred that her hair is long—there is nothing more in terms of a visual description.

Of course, Tenniel did have Carroll's original illustrations of Alice, and it's true that there is a certain resemblance between the two. An early version of Tenniel's Alice can be glimpsed in the pages of *Punch* in 1846—an illustration of a young, middle-class girl wearing a waisted dress and pinafore and placing a garland around the neck of a lion.

Tenniel is thought to have modeled the Duchess on Quentin Matsys' unflattering portrait. Titled *The Ugly Duchess,* it was painted around 1513.

Tenniel's drawing of Alice with the Duchess.

In other instances, Tenniel ignores Carroll's text and puts his own spin on a character. The Duchess that Alice meets in Chapter VI of *Alice in Wonderland* is described as having a chin that is "uncomfortably sharp," and when they walk together on the croquet grounds, the Duchess repeatedly digs her pointy chin into Alice's shoulder. Yet Tenniel's Duchess has a chin that is anything but sharp. But when Carroll also describes the Duchess as ugly, Tenniel doesn't fail the author. The Duchess is most definitely unattractive. Critics posit that Tenniel based the Duchess on the Duchess Margaret of Carinthia and Tyrol, who lived in the fourteenth century and was reputed to

be the ugliest woman in history. Quentin Matsys, a sixteenth-century Flemish painter, did a portrait of her that Tenniel very likely used as his inspiration.

Although Carroll almost certainly modeled the White Knight on himself, as discussed on page 14, Tenniel also laid claim to the errant knight, making the character—in a way—a metaphor for the collaboration between these two great artists. Tenniel's knight has the illustrator's trailing mustache, and the resemblance between the two is striking. Tenniel might also have been influenced by the German artist Albrecht Dürer's engraving *Knight, Death, and the Devil* (1513–14).

Critics remark on the similarities between Albrecht Dürer's engraving (above left) and Tenniel's White Knight (above right).

As expertly as Tenniel prepared the illustrations for both Alice books, he did make mistakes. In *Alice in Wonderland*, for instance, the illustration that opens Chapter I shows the White Rabbit in a checkered jacket over a plain vest. Yet later, when giant Alice is stuck inside the rabbit's house and reaches out through a window to grab hold of him, he is wearing a checkered vest to match his jacket. And in *Through the Looking-Glass* Tenniel mistakenly gives Tweedledee, not Tweedledum, the wooden sword.

After completing *Through the Looking-Glass*, Tenniel all but retired from illustrating books, concentrating instead on his political cartoons for *Punch*. He illustrated a handful of books for other authors, and in 1881, agreed to one last project from

Carroll—the colorized edition for *The Nursery Alice*. Tenniel made some substantial changes to some of the twenty illustrations that appear in the book. He updated Alice's costume, pleating her dress and adding a bow to the apron, and he placed another bow in her hair. He redid the frontispiece and redrew the illustration of Alice holding the "Drink Me" bottle as well as the one of her with a stretched-out neck.

Since the later book was intended for young children, the black-and-white illustrations were colorized. Alice was given a yellow dress, and blue bows and stockings. The Knave of Hearts had his nose painted red, a suggestion perhaps that he was a lush and under the influence of alcohol when he stole the King's tarts.

From Drawing to Printed Illustration

Tenniel completed his drawings for the Alice books during the height of the golden age of illustration in England. At this time, most illustrations were produced for printing using a process known as wood engraving. The method called for a division of labor between the artist and the engraver. After the artist had drawn his illustration, the engraver would prepare a cutting of the drawing—reversed left to right—on a block of wood. The cutting would appear in relief, the lines of the drawing standing out against the gouged-out background. When printed, the lines would print black against the white pages. The process allowed for highly detailed images; however, cutting out the many intricate lines and multiple crosshatchings required hours upon hours of tedious work for the engraver.

The professional engravers who worked on both Alice books were George and Edward Dalziel, known as the Brothers Dalziel. The family-owned business worked with a who's who of important nineteenth-century artists, including Dante Gabriel Rossetti and James McNeill Whistler. Although Carroll often took the brothers to task, finding fault with the engravings, he appeared satisfied in the end with their work. Along with a check, he sent a note that stated that he thought the pictures were "first-rate specimens of the art of wood-engraving."

Peter Newell (1862–1924)

Born the year that Lewis Carroll invented the story of Alice and her adventures underground, American Peter Newell grew up to become a freelance artist and writer, and the first major illustrator since Tenniel to interpret Carroll's works. At the turn of the century, Harper & Brothers Publishers selected him to illustrate three of Carroll's books: *Alice's Adventures in Wonderland*, *Through the Looking-Glass*, and *The Hunting of the Snark*, a long, nonsensical poem. For his Alice, Newell used his dark-haired daughter Jo as a model. When the book was published in 1901, the reading public was alarmed to discover Alice with dark locks.

In an article he wrote for an October 1901 issue of *Harper's Monthly Magazine*, Newell admits that Tenniel has captured Alice's character "in a way none may rival"; yet, he goes on in a vein of false modesty to allow that his own attempt to portray Alice "will not be altogether unwelcome." Newell envisioned Alice as "a sweet, childish spirit at home in the midst of mysteries," "a demure, quaint little girl, with a strict regard for the proprieties of life, and a delicate sense of consideration for the feelings of others . . . ." For Newell, Alice was a symbol of the purity of childhood, and his pencil drawings reveal a gentler, kinder Wonderland than Tenniel's edgier illustrations do.

Newell said of Alice, "The dominant note in the character of Alice is childish purity and sweetness."

Rackham copied the exact pattern on his wife's china for the tea setting in the Hatter's party.

Arthur Rackham (1867–1939)

In 1907, the copyright for *Alice's Adventures in Wonderland* expired and there was a mad rush by publishers to deliver new editions, most of them unremarkable and blatant in their slavish adherence to Tenniel's illustrations. One notable exception was Arthur Rackham's version. Rackham was already renowned for his book illustrations for *Rip Van Winkle* by Washington Irving and *Peter Pan in Kensington Gardens* by J. M. Barrie when the publishing house Heinemann commissioned him to illustrate *Alice in Wonderland*. His drawings, with their sinuous lines and muted, somber colors, were very different from Tenniel's. Rackham's Wonderland is ominous and foreboding, full of frightening trees with knotty trunks and twisty branches, and creatures with sharp beaks and claws.

Unlike Tenniel, Rackham used a model for his Alice—Doris Jane Dommett, who also posed for his

versions of Cinderella and Sleeping Beauty. Demure and reserved, this Alice shows none of the anger or fear of Tenniel's Alice; instead, she is sanguine and unaffected by her experiences, often remaining expressionless no matter what disturbing events are taking place around her. At the Hatter's tea party, she sits at the end of the long table, hand on her lap, as if she were at an ordinary society function and not in the midst of lunatics.

Rackham's *Alice in Wonderland* illustrations made use of a new technology that freed illustrators from having to have their artwork engraved on wood or metal plates before it could be printed. Book illustrations were photographed and reproduced mechanically instead. This advance greatly benefited Rackham, whose sinuous lines could now be rendered exactly as he had drawn them and didn't depend on an engraver's skill.

Rackham's illustrations for *Alice in Wonderland* were a success, with many critics praising his approach, while others continued to hold Tenniel's original drawings as the only true version. According to Derek Hudson in his biography of Rackham, *Alice in Wonderland* was "so completely identified with the drawings of John Tenniel that it seemed to many critics almost blasphemous for anyone to attempt to prepare alternatives."

Willy Pogany (1882–1955)

Born in Hungary, Willy Pogany lived in Munich, Paris, London, and New York City, all the while developing his artistic skills in whatever city he found himself. Besides being an illustrator, in his later years, he also worked as an art director on Hollywood films, and as a scenery and costume designer for the Metropolitan Opera House in New York City. A 1929 edition of *Alice in Wonderland,* heavily illustrated with his pen-and-ink drawings, has a bold, modern look, setting it apart from other, more mundane editions of the time.

Pogany's crisp, clean modern style is most obvious in the way that Alice is portrayed. Gone are Tenniel's prim frock and long, flowing hair; with her bobbed haircut and sporty outfit, Pogany's Alice resembles a Jazz Age flapper more than a cosseted little girl.

Mervyn Peake (1911–1968)

Mervyn Peake's quirky, dark illustrations for *Alice in Wonderland* and *Through the Looking-Glass* are a result, in part, of his disturbing experiences as a war artist at the end of World War II. In 1945, Peake, on assignment for *Leader* magazine, toured war-torn Germany and witnessed the devastation firsthand. He traveled to bombed-out cities such as Bonn and Cologne, visited a former concentration camp, and sketched a trial for war criminals. Peake also sketched the victims he saw suffering at the newly liberated Bergen-Belsen concentration camp. The horror of his experiences in Germany, at "this unutterable desolation," left an indelible mark on him.

The following year, while living on the island of Sark, one of the Channel Islands off the coast of France, he sketched the first of his drawings for *Alice in Wonderland*. A notable fantasy writer as well as an artist, Peake had already completed illustrations for Carroll's long, nonsensical poem *The Hunting of the Snark* (1941). His aim as an illustrator—he long claimed—was to forget himself and allow the work of the author to speak through his pen. Peake's Alice wanders through a dark and malevolent Wonderland, and the reader fears for her safety among its mad inhabitants. Peake's White Rabbit looks angry, his face in a scowl and his fists clenched, as he stomps toward the viewer. The writer Graham Greene hailed Peake as "the first artist since Tenniel to recast Alice in a contemporary mold." Unfortunately, it took the ravages of war for Peake to achieve this feat.

With her chic bob and checkered skirt, Alice reflects the styles of the Roaring Twenties in Willy Pogany's bold illustrations.

Peake's depiction of the White Rabbit, who appears angry with fists raised and eyebrows narrowed.

Titled *Who Stole the Tarts,* this illustration was created by Dalí for the penultimate chapter of *Alice in Wonderland.*

Ralph Steadman (1936–present)

A satirist best known for his illustrations for author Hunter S. Thompson, Ralph Steadman produced his first frenzied, ink-splattered illustrations in the madcap counter-culture of the mid-1960s, reflecting the turbulence of the times. In his introduction to the 1967 edition of *Alice in Wonderland*, Steadman notes how some of the major characters evolved and what they stand for. The anxious, ever-hurrying, always-late White Rabbit is the harried modern commuter. The Cheshire Cat is "an ideal TV Announcer whose smile remains as the rest of the program fades out." The playing-card gardeners are British trade unionists, "bickering about who splashed who and standing in the stuff all the time any way." Other modern-day references include Alice's "Drink Me" bottle configured as a classic bottle of Coke.

Steadman's Alice reacts dynamically to what she witnesses in her strange surroundings, often wearing a startled expression. In certain illustrations, Steadman portrays his heroine in the Cubist style, flattening and rearranging her as if she were in a painting by Picasso. In one dramatic spread, Alice is fitted contortionist-style into the White Rabbit's room. The interior is inky black and Alice's cramped figure stands out in bold relief.

Salvador Dalí (1904–1989)

The artist Salvador Dalí, famous for his surreal images of melting clocks and barren landscapes, at first glance might not seem to have much in common with a retiring Victorian English don who wrote children's books. But actually, Dalí and Carroll had much in common: both men were ardent explorers of dreams and the imagination, attempting in their art to show the fertile pathways to the unconscious.

This artistic temperament might explain why, in his sixties, Dalí created twelve surreal illustrations—one for each chapter—for *Alice in Wonderland*. Because he required a rich, lush palette for his painted drawings, Dalí turned to the oldest process for reproducing photographic images for printing: heliogravure. Similar to engraving, the method is time consuming and costly. Each heliogravure is printed by hand and considered an original. It is no surprise then that Dalí's completed book, published in 1969 by Maecenas Press–Random House, is a valuable commodity.

Max Ernst (1891–1976)

Another surrealist drawn to Carroll's Wonderland was Max Ernst. In his seventies, he created a series of lithographs for a 1970 German edition of a collection of Carroll's works entitled *Lewis Carroll's Wunderhorn.* The book included the Mad Tea Party excerpt from *Alice in Wonderland*. A true surrealist, Ernst wasn't interested in capturing a realistic interpretation of the party; instead, his three lithographs are composed of geometric patterns in various combinations.

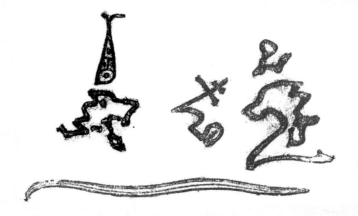

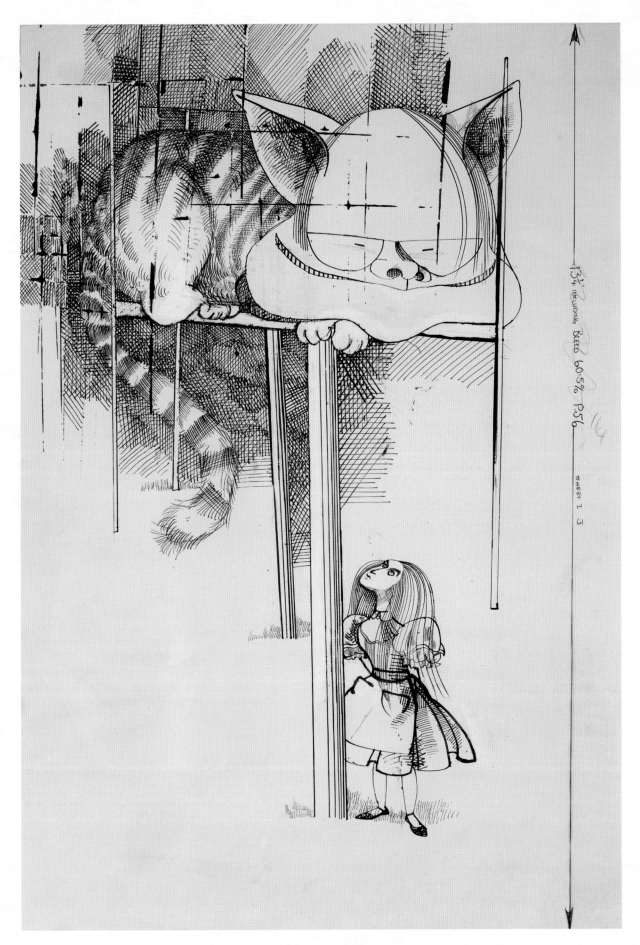

Steadman's interpretation of the Cheshire Cat as a television announcer.

Barry Moser (1940–present)

The model for the March Hare was a rabbit decapitated by the Moser family's pet cat.

Like Peter Newell, Barry Moser used a dark-haired daughter as his model for Alice. Maddy, his youngest of three daughters, bore an uncanny resemblance to Alice Liddell, the girl who inspired the story. Yet Moser's Alice appears in *Alice in Wonderland* only four times—before and after her dream. Moser's explanation for this unusual choice is that he wanted the reader to experience Wonderland through Alice's eyes.

A master wood engraver, Moser sketched hundreds of drawings before settling on the seventy-five that appear in the published book. Then he spent a good part of a year engraving the images into wood. The results are stunning, dramatic, and undeniably dark, like when the Cheshire Cat grins at the reader with razor-sharp teeth. Moser, who hadn't read *Alice in Wonderland* until he was a grown man, didn't see it as a children's story: "To me, it was a much darker tale, and I wanted people to see Wonderland the way Alice saw it—less whimsical and more nightmarish."

First published as a limited edition from his Pennyroyal Press, Moser's *Alice in Wonderland* won a National Book Award in 1983 for design and illustration. The following year, Moser published *Through the Looking-Glass* as a companion book. Like the first book, the woodcuts show us only what Alice sees in her adventures. Moser based many of the portraits on people he knew as well as on historical figures. The White Knight, for instance, was patterned after Lewis Carroll, and former U.S. President Richard Nixon served as Moser's inspiration for Humpty Dumpty.

Moser's engraving of Humpty Dumpty.

A worried-looking Mad Hatter holds his teacup upside down in Moser's deft portrait.

A genial Humpty Dumpty shakes hands with Alice in one of Oxenbury's illustrations from *Through the Looking-Glass*.

Helen Oxenbury (1938–present)

When it was published in 1999, Helen Oxenbury's *Alice in Wonderland* was met with almost unanimous rave reviews. Critics hailed its fresh approach, deeming its heroine "an Alice for the new millennium" and "an Alice accessible to all ages." The following year, the book, a labor of love that took Oxenbury three years to complete, was awarded the prestigious Kate Greenway Medal for "distinguished illustration" in the United Kingdom.

Generously illustrated with almost every spread adorned with either spot-art or a full-color painting, the book portrays a Wonderland free of malice and hostility. The cartoonlike beasts appear to have neither claws nor fangs, and Alice has no fear as she roams among them. The story's darker subtext has no place in Oxenbury's interpretation.

Oxenbury was determined to show Alice as a child of today: confident, spunky, upbeat, and never in serious danger. Even her clothes are modern. Gone are Tenniel's stiff petticoats with their crinoline, as Alice gambols in a short blue dress that doesn't curtail her movements.

After she finished *Alice in Wonderland*, Oxenbury figured she was done with Carroll and didn't intend to illustrate any more of his works. But that changed when she read *Through the Looking-Glass* and, impressed by how good it was, illustrated it as well.

In Oxenbury's true-to-life illustration, Alice gets ready to kick Bill, the Lizard, up the chimney.

Other Notable Illustrators

In the years since the first Alice book was published, there have been countless illustrators who have been inspired to interpret Carroll's fantastical world. It is impossible to list them all, but here are a few more who merit recognition.

Mabel Lucie Attwell (1879–1964)

Working in both watercolor and pen-and-ink, Mabel Lucie Attwell produced sentimental illustrations of childhood for magazines, books, and ephemera, such as postcards and greeting cards. She was extremely popular during the 1930s and beyond. In 1910, before commercial success hit, she illustrated an edition of *Alice in Wonderland* that portrays Alice as a rosy-cheeked cherub.

Gwynedd Hudson (1909–1935)

British artist and illustrator Gwynedd Hudson received her education at the Brighton School of Art. Best known for her illustrations for J.M. Barrie's *Peter Pan* and Carroll's *Alice in Wonderland*, Hudson favored a darker, more somber palette than her fellow Alice illustrators. In 1932, Hodder & Stoughton, a London publisher, issued an elaborate gift-book edition of *Alice in Wonderland* that features her illustrations.

Above: Peter Blake's 1971 *And To Show You I'm Not Proud.*
Right: Lisbeth Zwerger's *Queen of Hearts.*

Peter Blake (1932–present)

The English Pop Artist Peter Blake, perhaps best known for his iconic design for The Beatles' *Sgt. Pepper's Lonely Heart Club Band* album cover, illustrated a 1970 edition of *Alice in Wonderland.* Blake strove to re-create the make-believe world of childhood in his series of watercolors. His Alice is a photo-realistic, freckled-faced young lady who gazes seriously at the viewer from the book's cover.

Lisbeth Zwerger (1953–present)

Published the same year as Helen Oxenbury's version, Lisbeth Zwerger's 1999 *Alice in Wonderland* couldn't be more different. Austrian-born Zwerger, the 1990 winner of the prestigious Hans Christian Andersen Medal for her "lasting contribution to children's literature," delved into the psychological tensions in Carroll's story. Her characters wear deadpan faces and often seem oblivious to their surroundings.

CHAPTER 3
Alice on Stage

"The stage (as every playgoer can testify) is an engine of incalculable power for influencing society; and every effort to purify and ennoble its aims seems to me to deserve all the countenance that the great, and all the material help that the wealthy, can give it . . ."
—Lewis Carroll, 1882

As a clergyman, Lewis Carroll's father, Reverend Charles Dodgson, was prohibited by the Church of England from visiting the theater. Indeed, during Victorian times the theater was considered by many to be immoral and, therefore, a place to be avoided. Lewis Carroll, as we can see by the above quote, did not share these views. A devoted theatergoer throughout his life, he had a passion for plays, concerts, and operas, and kept a journal in which he documented the events he attended. He also befriended actors, such as Ellen Terry, a celebrated Shakespearean actress. Carroll was fortunate to live long enough to see the first stage production of *Alice's Adventures in Wonderland* and deem it a success. Since that first pantomime, a slew of creative artists have put forth their stage versions, including plays, operas, and ballets.

Alice in Wonderland: A Musical Dream Play, in Two Acts, for Children and Others

Adapted by Henry Savile Clark. 1886–1887.

In August of 1886, the playwright Henry Savile Clarke approached Carroll with a request for permission to adapt the two Alice books for the stage; specifically, Clarke wanted to make a pantomime, a distinctly British type of entertainment usually held around Christmastime. Based on a familiar tale, a pantomime includes music and slapstick comedy. Carroll, who years earlier had tried to drum up interest in a theatrical production, was receptive but cautious. In his reply, he stated that he had "…one, and only, one condition, which I should regard as absolutely essential before allowing my name to appear as 'sanctioning' any dramatic version…that I should have your written guarantee that, neither in the libretto nor in any of the stage business, shall any coarseness, or anything suggestive of coarseness, be admitted."

Carroll had a further series of requests: that the production not have a harlequinade (a harlequin-like clown common in pantomimes), that only one—not both—of the Alice stories be dramatized, and that for songs that were parodies "the old air should be used." Clarke agreed to omitting the harlequinade and using the old airs for the songs, but he stood his ground about basing the operetta on both books.

Carroll continued to poke his nose into the production, writing a stream of letters to Clarke offering suggestions. He even had an opinion on whom to cast in the role of Alice—Phoebe Carlo, a twelve-year-old actress friend of Carroll's. Clarke agreed to Carlo but nixed Carroll's wish to design the young lady's costume himself. Perhaps Carroll realized he was becoming too wrapped up in the production because in November, a month before the comic opera was to open, he wrote to Clarke stating that he was withdrawing his suggestions "en masse." He went on to write, "Amateurs have no business to put in their oar; it only spoils things."

Alice in Wonderland, the first professional production of Carroll's books, opened on December 23, 1886, at the London West End's Prince of Wales Theatre. In spite of his keen interest in the play, Carroll didn't see it until one week later. On opening day, he was traveling to his hometown of Guildford to spend Christmas with his sisters. When he did finally see the production, he wrote his "review" in his diary, giving praise to the first act and panning the second:

What Might Have Been

Ten years before the Alice pantomime was performed, Carroll approached Arthur Sullivan, the acclaimed composer, to set some of his poems in *Alice's Adventures in Wonderland* to music. Sullivan suggested that they collaborate and asked Carroll to write a full libretto for a musical production. Unfortunately, Carroll didn't think he was up to the task and turned him down.

Right: Phoebe Carlo, as Alice, poses with Dorothy d'Alcourt in her Dormouse costume.

Dec: 30. (Th). The first act ('Wonderland') goes well, specially the Mad Tea Party, Mr. Sydney Harcourt is a capital "Hatter", and little Dorothy d'Alcourt (aet. 6½) a delicious Dormouse. Phoebe Carlo is a splendid 'Alice'. Her song and dance with the Cheshire Cat (Master C. Adeson, who played the Pirate King in *Pirates of Penzance*) was a gem. The second act [*Through the Looking-Glass*] was flat. The two queens (two of the Rosa Troupe) were *very* bad (as they were also in the First Act as Queen and Cook): and the 'Walrus etc.' had no definite finale. But, as a whole, the play seems a success.

A success it was, both critically and at the box office. The *Daily News* praised its "sweet and wholesome combination of drollery and fancy, of humor and frolic, of picturesque beauty and brilliant pageantry"; the *Times* predicted it would become "a highly popular production"; and the *Daily Telegraph* assured its readers that audiences would "laugh till their sides ache." The production ran for fifty performances, closing on February 26, 1887.

Because the first production was such a success, Clarke proposed a revival, and on December 26, 1888, a new *Alice in Wonderland* opened at the Globe Theatre in London. Carroll felt that Phoebe Carlo was now too old for the part of Alice and expressed his concern to Clarke that by the end of the first production "…Phoebe was beginning to play mechanically." Ever eager to help with the casting, Carroll went to bat for another of his child actress friends, Isa Bowman, who, although born the same year as Carlo, looked younger and, according to Carroll, was "more of a lady than Phoebe." Bowman, who was convent-educated and the daughter of a music teacher, came from a higher social class than Carlo, the child of working-class parents. Bowman replaced Carlo, and Carroll wrote to Clarke about the new production that "…in many respects it is quite superior to the old one."

Alice in Wonderland

Written by Florida Friebus and Eva Le Gallienne. 1932, 1947, and 1982.

An accomplished actress, director, and producer, Eva Le Gallienne opened the Civic Repertory Theatre in downtown New York City, in 1926, in order to provide excellent theater at affordable prices. Le Gallienne succeeded in her goal, producing a number of plays by Henrik Ibsen, William Shakespeare, and other important dramatists. In the 1930s, with *Peter Pan* in the company's repertory, she wanted to do another play that would be attractive to both children and grownups, and adapted *Alice's Adventures in Wonderland* to the stage. As Le Gallienne wrote in her memoirs, "I decided to base our production on my firm conviction that *Alice in Wonderland* is by no means primarily for children. I am indeed inclined to believe the opposite to be true."

For the production, she and fellow actress Florida Friebus wrote the script, one that has been almost continually in print and is still used today by amateur theater companies throughout the world. According to an interview that Le Gallienne gave to the *New York Times* in 1982, the two women were determined "to make the book come alive, a heavy responsibility." She also claimed that "there's not a word in the play that's not Lewis Carroll's." The only changes to Carroll's works were the sequencing of certain episodes.

The set and costumes—"down to the smallest prop"—were faithful to Tenniel's original drawings as well. Because Le Gallienne thought it of utmost importance that Alice appear on stage at all times in order to establish continuous action, the set was devised as a cyclorama. The technique, quite sophisticated for its time, involved "a track laid horizontally across the stage upon which two medium-sized chariot platforms alternatively rode, shuttlewise, varied occasionally by the use of the full stage without platform, and backed by a roll of scenery (the cyclorama) that could be kept in constant motion at varying speeds." With such a setup, Alice could remain on stage for the entire performance while the scenery and characters came to her.

An actress as well as a dancer and choreographer, Bambi Lynn (performing here in the Friebus and Le Gallienne production of *Alice in Wonderland*) also performed in the original production of the musical *Oklahoma!* (1943) and *Carousel* (1945).

Kate Burton, in her Alice costume, poses with her father Richard Burton as the White Knight.

And how many characters there were! Le Gallienne's production, which she also directed, featured more than fifty cast members, with Le Gallienne herself taking on the role of the White Queen. Since Carroll, in *Through the Looking-Glass*, describes the Queen as being blown by the wind, Le Gallienne "flew" on and off the stage with the help of wires. Also included in the elaborate production were marionettes (for the Walrus and the Carpenter scene), and song-and-dance numbers.

The play opened on December 12, 1932, not long after Alice Hargreaves' visit to the United States to mark the centenary of Carroll's birth. Josephine Hutchinson starred as Alice and won rave reviews for her portrayal. She said that her interpretation came out of her mother's "cleanliness-is-next-to-godliness technique of dressing little girls."

Popular with audiences as well as critics, the production was a hit. The well-regarded *New York Times*' theater critic Brooks Atkinson described it in his review as "light, colorful and politely fantastic." He went on to write: "No doubt the children will love it if their imaginations are still unfettered. But it is certain that their elders will love it with a nostalgic rapture for the days that no longer come."

In 1947, the play was revived uptown at the International Theatre before moving to the Majestic Theatre, where it remained for most of its one hundred performances. Again, Le Gallienne directed as well as acted the part of the White Queen. Twenty-one-year-old Bambi Linn played Alice (see page 43). Several minor roles were taken on by two actors who would later go on to become stars of Hollywood and Broadway: Eli Wallach performed as both the Duck and the Two of Spades, while Julie Harris was an alternate for the White Rabbit.

In December 1982, fifty years after it was first performed, Le Gallienne's version of *Alice in Wonderland*

returned to the stage, on Broadway at New York City's Virginia Theatre. The production did not have a long run, totaling just twenty-one performances. Kate Burton played a "charmingly picture-book Alice," according to the *Christian Science Monitor*, and Le Gallienne, for the last time, reprised her role as the flying White Queen.

While the set and costumes were generally praised, critics did not react favorably to the play as a whole. Frank Rich, writing for the *New York Times*, called the revival flat, lamenting that it was "lifeless nearly from beginning to end."

Considering the bad reviews and its short run, it was all the more amazing when PBS's *Great Performances* decided to put on a production of the play for its 1983 season. Even more amazing was that the resulting television play was a success. Kate Burton returned to resume the part of Alice, but the rest of the cast was replaced with well-known actors, including Coleen Dewhurst (Red Queen), Maureen Stapleton (White Queen), Nathan Lane (Dormouse), and Donald O'Connor (Mock Turtle). Perhaps the biggest coup d'état was landing Richard Burton, Kate Burton's father, to play the role of the White Knight.

Besides a new cast, another major change to the televised production was the addition of a framework to bracket the play. The production, directed by Kirk Browning, opens with a nervous Kate Burton as an understudy about to go on stage as Alice. As she sits in her dressing room, she drifts into a private fantasy about the show, merging the personalities of the other members of the acting troupe with the *Alice in Wonderland* characters.

In a review, John J. O'Connor of the *New York Times* conceded that while the production is still not a great "Alice," many of the sketches are "marvelously executed."

Alice in Concert

Book, lyrics, and score by Elizabeth Swados. Directed by Joseph Papp. Choreographed by Graciela Daniele. 1980–1981.

Meryl Streep, fresh from her role as Joanna Kramer in *Kramer vs. Kramer*, was thirty-one years old in 1980, the year she took to the Public Theater's stage as Alice in *Alice in Concert*, Elizabeth Swados's musical adaptation of Lewis Carroll's Alice books. Wearing baggy, pastel overalls, her long blond hair in curls, Streep pouted and pranced her way through the production's thirty-plus musical numbers, having great fun in her role as a seven-year-old girl. For her unbridled performance, she won a 1980–1981 Obie Award.

Elizabeth Swados had spent seven years writing the production's book and musical score, giving Carroll's works a contemporary retelling. The songs comprise a variety of styles. The Mad Tea Party is set to a country-western tune; a number in which Alice says farewell to her feet is given a calypso beat. Other musical styles include blues, folk, tango, and even a barbershop quartet performance.

Directed by the Public Theater's founder, Joseph Papp, the production ran from December 9, 1980, to January 25, 1981. Besides Streep, there were a number of actors in the ensemble cast who would go on to have distinguished careers, including Mark Linn-Baker, Michael Jeter, and Amanda Plummer.

Staging and costumes for the production were minimal but effective. To portray the Caterpillar, for instance, several actors sat behind one another as they waved their arms to simulate the insect's many legs.

While reviews in general were favorable—especially of Streep's performance—there were dissenting opinions. The *New York Times* critic Frank Rich raved about Streep's Alice, calling her "a wonder." He also wrote, "This vague evening summons up so little of the letter or spirit of Carroll's nonsense tales that you must bring copies of the original texts to the Public just to follow what is going on."

John Simon, writing for *New York Magazine*, was even more biting in his appraisal of the production:

"Lewis Carroll scored doubly with his Alice books: He told rattling good tales for children and, simultaneously, logical conundrums, philosophical spoofs, and literary persiflage for adults. In *Alice in Concert*, Elizabeth Swados has jettisoned most of this and substituted an arrested sixties sensibility that undercuts Carroll, as hippies, flower children, potheads on a black linoleum floor welter and wallow, careen and cavort, trivializing or muffling whatever they touch."

Right: Production still of Meryl Streep as Alice from *Alice in Concert*.

Alice at the Palace

On January 16, 1982, NBC restaged Elizabeth Swados' musical as a made-for-television production for children entitled *Alice at the Palace*. Meryl Streep again starred as Alice, and many of the original cast returned as well. One new performer was Debbie Allen as the Red Queen.

Alice in Wonderland

Composed by Unsuk Chin. Libretto by David Henry Hwang and Unsuk Chin. 2007.

Born in Seoul, Korea, in 1961, Unsuk Chin, who moved to Berlin in 1988, studied under and was greatly influenced by György Ligeti, an important Hungarian composer of contemporary music. Ligeti's influence can especially be felt in Chin's first opera, *Alice in Wonderland*. For much of his professional career, Ligeti, whose favorite book was *Alice's Adventures in Wonderland*, intended to compose an opera of Carroll's classic but it never materialized. When Ligeti died in 2006, Chin decided to begin her own opera about Alice. With the playwright David Henry Hwang as her cowriter, she worked on the libretto. Beside the addition of a new introduction and ending, the text stays close to Carroll's original story, although there are occasional references to the modern world, as when the Dormouse inserts Mickey Mouse, Mao, and Marx into a list of words beginning with the letter M. Attracted to Carroll's dreamworld, Chin says, "I was fascinated and wholly amazed because I recognized much of what I had seen in my own dreams. I wanted the dreamworld to be the reality in my opera."

The opera had its premiere at the Bavarian State Opera in Munich in July 2007. Achim Freyer designed and directed the production, staging it with a huge cast of performers, many hidden behind huge cartoonish masks made from mesh. The English soprano Sally Matthews played Alice from under such a mask, leaving her expressionless; only through her movements and her voice could she convey emotion. Conducted by Kent Nagano, the opera was beautifully sung in English, the music calibrated to each Wonderland performer. Andrew Clements of the *Guardian* described Chin's music as "a palette of exquisite orchestral writing—the Mad Hatter's tea party becomes a *baroque scena*, the Caterpillar's advice is delivered as a bass-clarinet solo, and the Mock Turtle is accompanied by a melancholy mouth-organ."

Chin's opera made its U. S. premiere at the Opera Theatre of Saint Louis, in June 2012. The production, directed by James Robinson and conducted by Michael Christie, had a more conventional set and costumes than the Munich one.

The Royal Opera House has commissioned a second opera from Chin that will focus on Carroll's second book. *Alice Through the Looking-Glass*. It is set to make its premiere in the 2018/2019 season.

Alice in Wonderland

Written and composed by Peter Westergaard. 2008.

The American composer Peter Westergaard, a professor emeritus at Princeton University since 2001, had already tackled Shakespeare's *The Tempest* and Herman Melville's *Moby Dick* when he decided to write an opera based on Carroll's *Alice's Adventures in Wonderland.* Westergaard's quirky opera, his sixth, had its premiere on May 22, 2008, at Princeton University's Richardson Auditorium.

As the opera evolved, Westergaard, who also directed the production, made some decisions that set it apart from most contemporary operas. To start, even though he wanted to portray Wonderland's vast cast of characters, he didn't like cluttering up the stage with a large number of performers. His solution was to pare the performers down to seven but have them take on multiple roles, except for soprano Jennifer Winn, who played Alice.

The other decision that shaped the look and sound of the production was to eliminate the orchestra; instead, members of the cast, when not portraying their characters, performed in the background, singing the chorus and playing an assortment of musical instruments. Among the most prominent instruments were nineteenth-century handbells. Without an orchestra, the performers would normally have had a difficult time finding the proper pitch. Westergaard found that the handbells helped. "The bells are the stabilizing factor," he said in an interview. "They provide pitch anchors for the singers."

A rear projection system projected the scenery at different sizes, cleverly creating the illusion of Alice shrinking or growing taller. The minimal scenery resembled Tenniel's original illustrations in spirit, and the costumes—designed for quick changes—were based on Victorian fashion with the animal characters suggested by their headwear—the White Rabbit, for instance, is dressed in a tweed jacket with a ruffled shirt, and on top of his head are two bushy rabbit ears.

Westergaard's *Alice*, which closely follows Carroll's story, was intended for adults, not children. He was drawn to Carroll's Wonderland because of its odd population of characters. "Something a little bizarre is actually better for opera, which is already bizarre because people sing instead of speak," he stated. After its Princeton premiere, the opera was next performed the following month at the Symphony Space in New York City.

Jennifer Winn, as Alice, performs against a projected table that makes her appear small.

Alice's Adventures in Wonderland

Choreographed by Christopher Wheeldon. Scenario by Nicholas Wright. Music by Joby Talbot. 2011.

A tap-dancing Mad Hatter, a sixteen-legged Caterpillar, and a giant Cheshire Cat puppet made up of parts are just a few of the theatrical components in this dancing extravaganza. The first full-length ballet to have been created at the Royal Opera since 1995, *Alice's Adventures in Wonderland* had its premiere in London at the Royal Opera House in February 2011. The person commissioned to create the ballet was Christopher Wheeldon, an innovative choreographer who started his career at the Royal Ballet School before becoming the choreographer for the New York City Ballet. Nicholas Wright was the playwright/dramaturge, Joby Talbot provided the much-praised musical score, and Bob Crowley was responsible for the production's ingenious design.

For the most part, the ballet sticks closely to Carroll's original. One exception is the scene that opens the production: Set in the garden of the Liddell family's Oxford home, Alice, a teenager, and her two sisters listen to Lewis Carroll read them a story as guests mingle at a tea party. As in many Alice adaptations, the guests are stand-ins for the characters she will meet in Wonderland. Later, while photographing Alice, Carroll is transformed into the White Rabbit and Alice follows him—not down a rabbit hole, but through his camera bag into Wonderland.

Alice, as danced by Lauren Cuthbertson, then pirouettes, jetés, and pliés her way through the fantastical land. During her journey, she meets the inhabitants, one of whom is the vengeful Queen of Hearts played by Zenaida Yanowsky. In one of the ballet's more notable scenes, Yanowsky performs a parody of the famous Rose Adagio from *Swan Lake*. In another episode, the Duchess (danced by a man, the actor Simon Russell Beale) and a deranged cook (Kristen McNally) do battle in a kitchen that—with butchered hogs dangling from the ceiling—resembles a sausage factory. When Alice takes the howling baby from the Duchess it turns into a pig, and its fate can easily be guessed.

Reviews for the performances were overwhelmingly positive. Judith Mackrell of the *Guardian* summed it up best, when she stated: "[Wheeldon] and his team have created an Alice whose wit, speed and invention have lifted the whole story ballet genre into the 21st century." One recurring critique, though, was the overly long first act, which ran to seventy minutes. Other reviewers, while giving Cuthbertson full marks as a compelling Alice, conceded that her part was largely reactive. Many voiced the concern that *Alice in Wonderland* didn't have a "dance-friendly" plot. Luke Jennings, writing for the *Guardian*, said, "But Carroll's book is problematic. It depends to a considerable degree on wordplay, untranslatable into dance. There's no dramatic through-line, no character development, and, emotionally speaking, Alice remains a curiously disengaged figure throughout."

Left: Simon Russell Beale, in his role as the Duchess, shares a moment with Alice, played by Lauren Cuthbertson.

CHAPTER 4

Alice on the Big Screen

"I've seen mostly everything, but there's never been a version for me that particularly works, that I especially like or that blows me away."

—Director Tim Burton on *Alice in Wonderland* film adaptations

While Lewis Carroll was fortunate enough to see Alice traipse about on the stage, he didn't live long enough to see his creation on the cinema screen. Carroll died five years before the first *Alice in Wonderland* appeared on film in 1903. Since that time, a seemingly endless number of film adaptations have been made, with each producer or director interpreting Alice in his own way. The first three were silent movies. Audiences had to wait until 1931 to hear Alice speak. The 1930s saw a revival of interest in all things Alice, in large part due to the centennial of Carroll's birth in 1932. A major film to come out of the celebration was Paramount's 1933 extravaganza, full of Hollywood stars.

In the early days of film, directors struggled to produce— some successfully, others not—the visual effects that *Alice in Wonderland* demanded. By the time Tim Burton was ready to try his hand, technology allowed him to achieve effects unimaginable in the early years of the twentieth century. If Lewis Carroll were alive today, he'd surely be amazed— and, as an upstanding member of the clergy, in some cases horrified—at what his creation has brought forth.

Alice in Wonderland

Hepworth Studios. Directed by Cecil Hepworth and Percy Stow. 1903.

Produced in 1903, thirty-seven years after *Alice's Adventures in Wonderland* was published, Hepworth Studio's silent movie was very much a family affair. Hepworth, one of the film's directors, cast his wife in the roles of the Red Queen and the White Rabbit, and himself as the Frog Footman. Alice was played by May Clark (see page 55), the company's production secretary and general gofer. Even the Hepworth's pets got into the act—Alice encounters the Hepworth family dog when she enters Wonderland's garden, and the family's cat is the Cheshire Cat.

Cinema's first motion-picture version of Carroll's book runs a mere twelve minutes, yet it was the longest film produced in Britain at the time. The average British film in 1903 ran for about four minutes, so Hepworth's version was quite an epic, considering. Even so, twelve minutes couldn't begin to cover all of Alice's adventures, which wasn't a big problem because it was assumed that the audience was already familiar with the story. The film is more an illustration of the classic than a narrative.

The film begins with Alice asleep outdoors, dreaming that she sees the White Rabbit, whom she follows down a rabbit hole and through a narrow passage. She then enters the Hallway of Doors and, after growing and shrinking, proceeds through a tiny door and into a lush garden where she encounters a big dog. The next scene abruptly places her inside the White Rabbit's tiny house, back to her normal size and struggling to get out.

Other scenes portray Alice rescuing the Duchess' baby (who promptly turns into a pig); attending the Mad Tea Party, viewing a procession of playing cards, and playing croquet with the Queen of Hearts. The film ends with Alice offending the Queen, who calls for the executioner to cut off her head. Alice boxes the gentleman's ears and runs away. She wakes up, realizing that her adventures were just a dream.

The film attempted to stay true to John Tenniel's illustrations and largely it succeeds. The Hatter is almost the spitting image of Tenniel's drawings, and the costumes for the playing cards are painted according to the illustrator's exact designs. The film was made on a wooden stage in the garden of a house the company leased and used as their studio. The sets are little more than painted flats. Chairs, tables, and other furniture were borrowed from relatives and neighbors.

Credible visual effects also make this first version memorable. Filmgoers must have watched in awe as Alice grew and shrunk before their eyes in the Hallway of Many Doors. Although trick photography was common in films by 1903, most effects were the result of stage settings and optical illusions commonly used in the theater. In Hepworth's adaptation, by contrast, Alice's size changes were achieved through photographic means, most probably by superimposing two films. Audiences also got to see Alice crammed into the White Rabbit's house, her huge arm sticking out of one of the windows, and the metamorphosis of a baby in her arms into a piglet. Another visual effect shows the Cheshire Cat appearing magically in the branches of a tree, although, truth be told, the creature looks supremely bored.

Alice (May Clark) watches as a pack of playing cards parade past.

The Era of Nickelodeons

Because silent films didn't rely on language to be understood, they played throughout Europe and America. In England, people went to small theaters called "electric palaces" or "bioscope theaters" to watch them; in America, similar theaters, called "nickelodeons" (because admittance cost a nickel), existed. Hepworth's Alice made it across the pond in 1904, where it was released by the Edison Manufacturing Company and showed in such theaters. But because of its episodic nature, the film wasn't always shown in its entirety. Theater owners who preferred to feature a variety of film subjects would elect to buy one section, such as Alice's entry into Wonderland or the Mad Tea Party.

The British Film Institute has preserved the film and made it available online. Unfortunately, only fourteen of the original sixteen scenes have survived, and the film is badly damaged in parts, but it is still worthwhile to watch.

Move Over, Lassie

Two years after the Hepworth family's dog, Blair, made his appearance in *Alice in Wonderland*, he was cast again in *Rescue by Rover*. The film, which runs a little over six minutes, tells the story of how Rover finds and rescues a kidnapped baby girl. Although the film cost Hepworth only thirty-seven dollars to produce, it made him a rich man. The film was so popular that the negative wore out and Hepworth had to reshoot it. Then the second set wore out as well and he had to remake the film a third time. Blair went on to star in other films, becoming the first canine film star.

Alice's Adventures in Wonderland (A Fairy Comedy)

Edison Manufacturing Company. 1910.

The *New York Dramatic Mirror*, a theatrical trade paper, declared the first American screen production of *Alice Adventures in Wonderland (A Fairy Comedy)* "the most original and the most interesting film that has appeared in many a day." The one-reel silent film lasted ten minutes and starred the pint-sized Gladys Hulette as a brunette Alice. Filmed in New York City, in the Bronx, the movie contained fourteen scenes, one of which showed the Knave of Hearts stealing the tarts. Alice witnessed the act but later refuses to testify against him in the trial scene. The theft doesn't occur in Carroll's classic, although doubts are cast about his innocence. Unfortunately, no copies of the film exist today.

Alice in Wonderland

American Film Manufacturing Company. Written and directed by W. W. Young. 1915.

The third *Alice in Wonderland* filmed is this 1915 full-length production that clocks in at fifty-two minutes, again almost an epic by the standards of the time. Even so, the silent film, starring Viola Savory, a former stage actress, as Alice, does not include key episodes from Carroll's book. The most notable omission is the Mad Tea Party. Oddly, W. W. Young, its director, chose to include, in its entirety, one of the book's poems—the Caterpillar has Alice recite "Father Williams," and each verse is enacted on the screen.

As in most silent films, title cards cue the action. One of the most telling cards occurs at the beginning of the film: "Things we do and things we see shortly before we fall asleep are most apt to influence our dreams."

Puttin' on the Ritz

Although not an adaptation of *Alice's Adventures in Wonderland*, this 1930 film—shot in "glorious Technicolor"—about the rise and fall of a showbiz star (Harry Richman) devotes a six-minute song-and-dance sequence to *Alice's Adventures in Wonderland*. Coming at the end of the film, Joan Bennett, as Alice, performs to music and lyrics by Irving Berlin. In a February 15, 1930, *New York Times* review of the movie, critic Mordaunt Hall wrote:

"And then to cap the climax, there is the joyous sequence of 'Alice in Wonderland,' with a saucy rabbit smacking a lion on the jowl and Alice peering in the looking-glass. It is in this series of scenes that Miss Bennett sings 'With You,' in low, agreeable tones. Throughout this film she reveals herself to be a wonderful young actress, but, if anything, her expression is more captivating when she is rendering this melody than during the other none too imaginative interludes."

Young also neglected to show Alice's changes in size occurring in the moment; instead, she does all her shrinking and growing off-camera. His avoidance of special effects is puzzling, especially since these changes were managed a dozen years earlier in Hepworth and Stowe's production.

One aspect that Young absolutely got right was the costuming. The look of the film is pure Tenniel. Alice is dressed exactly to his specifications, and the White Rabbit is wearing the familiar checkered jacket. Even the Dodo makes its appearance complete with Tenniel's walking stick.

The film's outdoor scenes were filmed in Long Island, New York, and Cape Ann, Massachusetts.

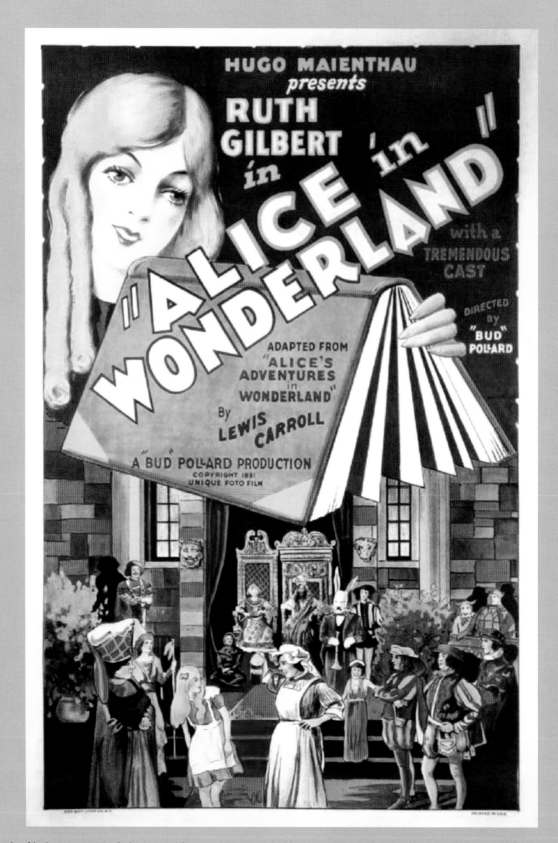

The film's opening and closing credits are accompanied by a rendition of the song "Come Along with Alice," which Irving Berlin wrote for *Century Girl*, a 1916 Broadway musical.

Alice in Wonderland

Metropolitan Studios. Directed by Bud Pollard. 1931.

Metropolitan Studios' 1931 production is distinguished by being the first version of an *Alice in Wonderland* film to offer sound. In the early 1930s, sound was just being introduced, and the film studio, based in Fort Lee, New Jersey, chose Carroll's book to adapt using the latest technology. That said, the production, clocking in at just under an hour, is a low-budget affair with a cast of amateurs who struggle to speak with British accents.

Eighteen-year-old Ruth Gilbert played Alice in her first major role. (In the 1950s, she became known for playing a scatterbrain secretary on *The Milton Berle Show*.) With her long blond wig, heavy makeup, and overarched eyebrows, Gilbert's Alice looks more like an overeager Lolita than a demure Victorian child, and more often than not, her New York accent breaks through her posh British accent.

For the most part, the film's storyline adheres to Carroll's book, although many of the episodes are abridged. One exception is the ending: The trial takes place, but the White Rabbit confesses to stealing the tarts and is sentenced to death. Even more oddly, it's hinted at that he is in love with the Duchess! Alice objects to his sentencing and, as in the book, the cards attack her before she awakes.

The film had its official premiere on December 25, 1931, at the prestigious Warner Theater in New York City's Times Square. As an added incentive to attend, free toys were handed out to children. Despite being the first talkie version of *Alice in Wonderland*, the film did not do well at the box office. In an unusual move, it was then released in nontheatrical venues, such as schools and churches, most likely to recoup production costs.

In its December 28, 1931, review, the *New York Times* was kind in its critique, stating, "There is an earnestness about the direction and the acting that elicit sympathy." It concluded its review with: "And although none of the acting is any too good, it will probably meet with favor from youngsters who go to see an articulate Alice on the screen."

Alice in Wonderland

Paramount Pictures. Directed by Norman McLeod. 1933.

Paramount pulled out its big guns when the studio adapted Carroll's Alice books to the screen in 1933. Leading film stars W. C. Fields, Gary Cooper, and Cary Grant were cast as Humpty Dumpty, the White Knight, and the Mock Turtle, respectively. Other top names—not as well known today but big in their day—include Edward Everett Horton (the Hatter), Charlie Ruggles (the March Hare), Richard Arlen (the Cheshire Cat), May Robson (the Queen of Hearts), and Edna May Oliver (the Red Queen).

Despite having such a stellar cast, Paramount seemed to go out of its way to make its stars unrecognizable.

Buried under heavy makeup or clunky and concealing costumes, the actors struggle to make their presences felt. Viewers have to take it on faith that Cary Grant is indeed inside the Mock Turtle costume. (Bing Crosby passed on the role.) For certain characters, the rigid masks make it difficult for the actors to say their lines or act with expression. One notable exception is W. C. Fields. His distinctive delivery and grouchy humor as the cantankerous Humpty Dumpty is a delight to watch.

The part of Alice went to Charlotte Henry, a relative unknown at the time. Henry was cast after Paramount auditioned more than 6,800 applicants. According to the film's producers and director, she landed the role because she was "just the type." With her long blond hair, slight build, and pretty features, twenty-year-old Henry does resemble Tenniel's Alice to an amazing degree.

Above: W. C. Fields was unrecognizable as Humpty Dumpty. Only his distinctive nasal drawl gave the actor away.
Right: Charlotte Henry, playing Alice in the 1933 film, was seventeen when she was selected for the part of Alice.

Although the costumes obscure many of the actors, they are impressive, as are the special effects. Some of the more innovative special effects include the hallway scene where Alice grows and shrinks, and the scene where the Cheshire Cat dissolves, leaving behind just its luminous grin. A somewhat alarming special effect occurs when Alice leaves the Duchess' house with the squalling baby (played by Billy Barty, a dwarf) only to have it change into a pig. In this movie version, the transformation is convincingly and even disturbingly conveyed.

The film was not a box office success, nor was it nominated for any Academy Awards. One person who did give the film a thumbs-up, calling it "a revolution in cinema history," was the original Alice. Mrs. Reginald Hargreaves, nee Alice Liddell, declared, "I am delighted with the film and am now convinced that only through the medium of the talking picture could this delicious fantasy be faithfully interpreted."

Far left: Cary Grant, standing next to his costume, was barely recognizable as the Mock Turtle in the 1933 production.

Alice's Adventures in Wonderland

Shepperton Studios, UK. Directed by William Sterling. 1972.

Josef Shaftel's lavish production of *Alice in Wonderland*, which marked the centenary of when Carroll completed *Through the Looking-Glass*, is remarkably accurate to the original text. Filmed in wide-screen Technicolor, and visually stunning, the live-action musical stays faithful to Carroll's dialogue and Tenniel's illustrations. The storyline sticks mainly to the first book, although Tweedledee and Tweedledum make an appearance earlier than in the book. The film is framed with the reenactment of the famous boat ride Carroll took with the Liddell sisters in 1862. On the riverbank, Carroll (played by Michael Jayston) begins to tell the story of Wonderland to Alice, who drifts off to sleep while listening to him.

Alice is played by Fiona Fullerton, who was fifteen years old at the time of filming. Fullerton, who later played a Bond girl in *A View to a Kill*, was cast because she looked so much like Tenniel's Alice. While that is true, she was also double the age that Carroll had intended Alice to be. The rest of the cast is made up of many notable British stars including Michael Crawford (the White Rabbit), Peter Sellers (the March Hare), Dudley Moore (the Dormouse), and Ralph Richardson (the Caterpillar).

As a musical, the songs on the whole tend to fall flat and the dance numbers are awkward. The film was not particularly well received in England or the United States, although it was awarded two BAFTA Awards (British Academy of Film and Television Arts) for cinematography and costume design.

Alice (Fiona Fullerton) at the Mad Tea Party with the Mad Hatter (Robert Helpmann), March Hare (Peter Sellers), and Dormouse (Dudley Moore).

X-Rated Alice

During the golden age of porn (1972–1983) nothing was off-limits, not even Carroll's fantasy for children. In 1976, director Bud Townsend had Alice (Kristine DeBell) interacting with the inhabitants of Wonderland like never before in his soft-porn film *Alice in Wonderland: An X-Rated Musical Comedy*. Alice is a librarian when we meet her, innocent and virginal. The mechanic she is in love with is upset when she spurns his advances and leaves. Alice then thumbs through Carroll's *Alice in Wonderland*, and before long, the White Rabbit appears and leads her through the looking-glass and into Wonderland. Lewis Carroll never imagined a Wonderland like this, with a dominatrix Queen of Hearts and a lecherous Hatter. Reviewing the movie on November 24, 1976, no less an esteemed film critic than Roger Ebert stated that it was "an X-rated musical comedy that actually has some wit and style to it." Ebert was especially taken with DeBelle, who "projects such a freshness and naiveté that she charms us even in scenes where some rather alarming things are going on."

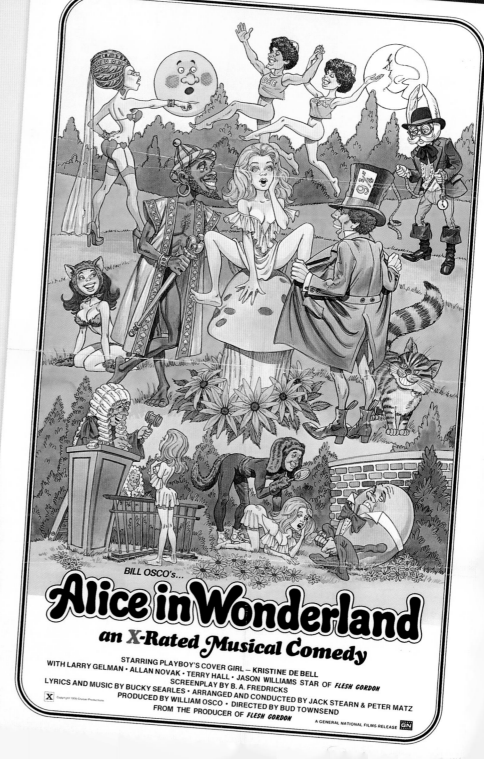

Jabberwocky

While not an adaptation of Carroll's novel, 1977's *Jabberwocky*, directed by Terry Gilliam of Monty Python fame, takes its central inspiration from Carroll's nonsense poem of the same name, which appears in *Through the Looking-Glass.* The movie, set sometime during the Dark Ages, follows a naïve apprentice (played by Michael Palin, another member of the Monty Python troupe), as he gets into one misadventure after another before vanquishing the ferocious beast. In spite of being the titular character, the monster doesn't make an appearance until the final five minutes of the film.

To achieve the creature's monstrous appearance, Gilliam didn't rely on spectacular, cutting-edge special effects; instead, the man playing the monster donned the costume, with its freakishly long neck—controlled like a marionette with poles and lines—and walked backward. The monster's jerky, awkward movements and winglike arms look disturbingly real; it's an old trick, and one used in the Godzilla movies of the 1950s. As Gilliam said, "Whenever I've asked people how they thought it was done, no one ever thought it was a guy walking with his back to the audience. It is so simple that no one ever realized. Many good effects are usually quite simple."

Above: Coral Browne playing Alice Liddell Hargreaves with the Mad Hatter and the March Hare in *Dreamchild*.

Below: Hargreaves approaches the Tortoise (left) and Gryphon (right) in one of the early dream sequences.

Dreamchild

EMI Films. Directed by Gavin Miller. 1985.

Based in part on the real-life trip Alice Liddell Hargreaves took in 1932, when she traveled to New York City to receive an honorary degree from Columbia University, *Dreamchild* is concerned with memory and the realization of one's mortality. Penned by Dennis Potter, who in 1965 also wrote the teleplay *Alice* as part of the BBC's *The Wednesday Play* series, the film deftly shows how the elderly Hargreaves (Coral Browne) is unnerved by the brash hordes of journalists who descend upon her after her ocean liner pulls into New York's harbor. Hargreaves is distressed when the reporters impertinently call her "Alice" and bombard her with questions. Her young and timid servant, and traveling companion, Lucy (Nicola Cowper), is no match for the reporters either, and is fooled into letting one of them into the hotel room. Jack Dolan (Peter Gallagher) manages to wrangle his way into their lives and, predictably, into Lucy's heart.

As Hargreaves becomes overwhelmed by the hoopla over her arrival and her newfound celebrity, she revisits the years when she knew Lewis Carroll and their relationship, events she hasn't thought about in decades. Through flashbacks and dreams, we see young Alice (Amelia Shankley) and Carroll (Ian Holm) together; Alice, portrayed as precocious and lively, is frequently impertinent toward Carroll, splashing him with water on a boat ride or teasing him about his stutter. Holm's repressed Carroll remains devoted to her, though, no matter how she behaves.

At times, Hargreaves's memories veer into the fantastical, as she imagines herself in Carroll's Wonderland. In some of the film's most effective and surreal scenes, Hargreaves appears as young Alice being interrogated by Wonderland characters until she abruptly changes into her elderly self. Only six Wonderland characters appear—the Gryphon, the Mock Turtle, the Hatter, the March Hare, the Dormouse, and the Caterpillar—but all are frightening and sinister. The March Hare with his yellowing teeth derides her for her foolishness; the Caterpillar reminds her, "You are old, Mrs. Hargreaves." Jim Henson's Creature Shop designed and built the puppets, which were based on Tenniel's original illustrations.

Hargreaves's memories ultimately cause her to realize how her childish taunts hurt the sensitive author and reveal to her the depth of his love for her. The film skirts the issue of whether his love is erotically charged. His behavior, though, is always proper, if not stiff.

While *Dreamchild* did not have a long life at the box office, its reviews were generally favorable, especially with regard to Coral Browne's performance: she was named Best Actress by the Evening Standard British Film Awards. Ian Holm was also singled out for praise: as Pauline Kael noted, he "has to achieve almost all his effects passively, by recognizing the man's acute and agonizing self-consciousness and his furtive reactions to what goes on around him; it's all there in Holm's performance." In a more recent appreciation of the film, Lizzie Francke, writing in the *Guardian*, said of *Dreamchild* that it "…is a film with a powerful undertow that believes in the fantastical to explore the chaos of love, an emotion that disturbs as much as delights."

Alice Hargreaves's Trip to the New World

In 1932, to mark the centenary of Carroll's birth, Alice Liddell Hargreaves visited the United States, where she received an honorary doctorate from Columbia University. As in the film *Dreamchild*, she traveled by ocean liner; unlike the film, she didn't have a paid companion with her but was escorted by her sister and her youngest son. In a newsreel clip filmed during her stay, Hargreaves, who celebrated her eightieth birthday in New York City, says of Carroll: "I only remember him vaguely. I recall that he was the kindest of people to young children."

Alice Hargreaves, age eighty, during her visit to America.

Alice in Wonderland

Walt Disney Pictures. Directed by Tim Burton. 2010.

As Tim Burton tells it, there's never been an adaptation of *Alice in Wonderland* that particularly works, at least none that he has sat through, and each version "always ends up seeming like a clueless little girl wandering around with a bunch of weirdos." Determined to turn the Alice books' episodic nature into a cohesive film with a strong narrative, the director of such macabre and fantastical works as *Edward Scissorhands* and *The Nightmare Before Christmas* was drawn to screenwriter Linda Woolverton's action-packed script. The 3-D movie was put in motion by Woolverton's musings one day about what might happen if an older Alice returned to Wonderland. From this fledgling thought came a first draft of the script. Soon after, Disney came on board and hired Burton as the director; he and Woolverton worked together closely as they fleshed out and developed the script. In an interview with the *Guardian*, Burton commented, "Beyond all the kooky bells and whistles of my Alice, it's a simple story about somebody finding their own strength."

When, after a delay of more than a year, the completed film premiered in London on February 25, 2010, the audience saw not another staid adaptation of *Alice in Wonderland* but a stirring sequel in which nineteen-year-old Alice Kingsleigh returns to the underground fantasy world and discovers who she is and what she's made of. Played by the Australian actress Mia Wasikowska, Alice is a dreamy, introspective Victorian young lady when we first meet her. Plagued by disturbing dreams since childhood, she doesn't remember her first visit to Wonderland, known to its residents as Underland.

When creating her protagonist, Woolverton set about making her strong-willed and empowered. As she wrote her script she "did a lot of research on Victorian mores, on how young girls were supposed to behave, and then did exactly the opposite." Early on in the film, Alice is in a horse-drawn carriage with her mother, who is shocked to discover she has neglected to wear a corset or put on stockings. Later, at the garden party arranged for the public wedding proposal by the host's son, an insufferable aristocratic prig, Alice runs away to chase the White Rabbit rather than accepting the marriage that will imprison her.

A promotional poster for Tim Burton's *Alice in Wonderland*.

Top left: A promotional poster for Tim Burton's *Alice in Wonderland*.

Top right: Tim Burton and Helena Bonham Carter arrive at the French premiere of *Alice in Wonderland*, Paris.

Right: Fans showing off their elaborate costumes at Comic Con.

After tumbling down the rabbit hole, Alice finds herself once again in Underland. Believing herself to be in another one of her disturbing dreams, she is convinced she will soon wake up, so she doesn't take seriously the argument happening among a group of Underland characters as to whether she is the Alice whom it has been foretold will slay the Red Queen's Jabberwock, a beast that is wreaking havoc on the land. After being pursued by the Red Queen's minions, Alice finally makes her way to the Queen's palace to rescue the Hatter, who has sacrificed himself to allow Alice to escape.

Throughout her ordeals, she insists that she will not go up against the Jabberwock, but, of course, by the end of the film, dressed like a female version of Saint George slaying the dragon, she does just that, ridding the land of the beast and therefore the Red Queen, restoring rule to her sister, the White Queen. Her work over, Alice returns to the garden party a changed woman, one who stands up to her family and well-meaning friends, and refuses her suitor. The last the audience sees of her, she is standing on the deck of a trading ship, bound for Hong Kong and adventure.

The film is populated with an assortment of Carroll's Wonderland and Looking-Glass characters, such as Tweedledee and Tweedledum, the Caterpillar, the Cheshire Cat, and the Bandersnatch, a ferocious doglike creature. Johnny Depp, an actor who has appeared in a number of Burton's films, took on the role of the Hatter. With his electrifying green eyes and wild orange hair, the Hatter is mercurial—his moods, his appearance, and even his accent fluctuating at the drop of a hat. In preparing for the role, Depp researched Victorian hat makers, learning how they sometimes went mad as a result of the toxic mercury used to transform animal pelts into felt, which was then used to line hats. The disease caused the afflicted to undergo extreme mood changes: one minute they experienced rage, the next hilarity. Because the felting process, called carroting, caused the fur to turn orange, Depp requested that the Hatter's hair be orange as well.

Helena Bonham Carter played the Red Queen, an amalgamation of Carroll's Queen of Hearts and Red Queen. With her red lipstick applied in a heart shape and her gigantic, digitally altered head, the Red Queen rules Underland with a complete and total selfishness. Bonham Carter got her inspiration for the character from her then two-year-old daughter, Nell.

Visually stunning, Tim Burton's sequel is a special-effects extravaganza. Live actors; regular and CGI animation; and part-animated, part-human characters are combined to create a cohesive whole. Among the challenges facing Ken Ralston, the film's senior visual-effects supervisor, and his team were filming the Red Queen's abnormally large head so that the proportions worked in relation to the rest of her body; manipulating the Hatter's appearance to reflect his ever-changing mood swings; and having to shoot each scene Tweedledee and Tweedledum appeared in twice (the two were played by one actor, Matt Lucas). For the cast, the challenge was working so many hours on a green screen. Everything in Underland was shot on a green screen, and long exposure to being surrounded by so much green caused the cast and crew to feel sick and fatigued. Tim Burton's solution was to hand out lavender-tinted glasses to offset the green. After all the scenes were shot and complete, the film had to be converted into 3-D post-production. According to Ralston, the decision to use 3-D "was an additional tool to help an audience feel that Alice was spatially in some of these weird worlds we were creating."

With most critics praising the film's visual appeal—it went on to win Academy Awards for Best Art Direction and Best Costume Design—overall, *Alice in Wonderland* received mixed reviews. Todd McCarthy's *Variety* review is typical of many, stating, "…for all its clever design, beguiling creatures and witty actors, the picture feels far more conventional than it should; it's a Disney film illustrated by Burton, rather than a Burton film that happens to be released by Disney." Still, while the film wasn't a critic's darling, it generated more than a billion dollars worldwide, making it (as of this writing) the fifteenth-highest-grossing film of all time. With such box office influx, it's no wonder that a sequel is in the works. James Bobin, the director of the recent Muppet movies, not Burton, will be the director, and the film is due to be released in May 2016.

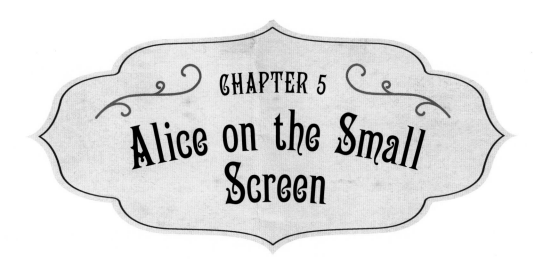

CHAPTER 5
Alice on the Small Screen

"Wonderland is a place where extraordinary and amazing things happen in the original book but also very dark and frightening things happen. In our world, it is now possible to act in ways which may seem strange and insane but are part of the norm. I do think that one of the things about our world is that we have advanced technology to such a point where we can get what we want to get when we want to get it. We can get somebody on the phone. We can watch a TV program when we want to watch a TV program. And we can enter into worlds of fantasy at the touch of a button. That certainly wasn't possible when Lewis Carroll wrote that book 150 years ago."

**—Director Nick Willing in an interview with Lisa Steinberg
for** *Starry Constellation Magazine*

As the quote above mentions, it wasn't possible in Lewis Carroll's day to turn on the television and have hundreds of programs instantly available. What would he have made of the many productions adapted from his books that have found their way directly into our homes on television screens?

The first televised adaptations of *Alice in Wonderland* appeared on flickering black-and-white screens. Years later, such television plays and specials are shown in glorious Technicolor, and today of course, viewers can watch any number of productions on all types of screens—TV, computer, tablets, or even phones. While the technology behind television viewing is ever changing, one thing remains constant: adaptations of the Alice books continue to appear on the small screen.

Early Adaptations

The first televised *Alice in Wonderland* appeared on the BBC series *Theatre Parade* in December 1937. Produced and directed by George More O'Ferrall, it showed scenes from a then-current West End play. (In January of that year, the series presented *Alice Through the Looking-Glass*, making it the first of Carroll's Alice books to appear on the small screen.) The next *Alice in Wonderland* television production wasn't until 1946. Again, O'Ferrall directed the BBC show, broadcast live from London's Alexandra Palace, and Alice was played by fourteen-year-old Vivian Pickles, who went on to have a distinguished career in both stage and film. In the 1950s, several adaptations were broadcast, including a live 1954 drama presented by Kraft Television Theater. Titled *Charlie McCarthy in Alice in Wonderland*, the show featured ventriloquist Edgar Bergen and his puppet Charlie as the pair narrated Alice's story. A young Art Carney played the Mad Hatter. In 1955, Hallmark Hall of Fame broadcasted in color a ninety-minute live production of *Alice in Wonderland*. The show was a staging of the 1932 play written by Florida Friebus and Eva Le Gallienne, who played her signature role of the White Queen (see page 42).

Alice

BBC. Directed by Gareth Davies. 1965.
A BBC production and a part of its acclaimed *The Wednesday Play* series, *Alice* is the fictionalized story of the relationship between Lewis Carroll and the young Alice Liddell. Written by Dennis Potter, a British television dramatist best known for *Pennies from Heaven* (1978) and *The Singing Detective* (1986), the show highlights Carroll's unrequited love for Alice. George Baker, who played Carroll, does a remarkable job of bringing the shy, stammering don to life. As a bonus, the actor resembles Carroll to an uncanny degree. The film begins when Alice is about ten years old, just before Carroll writes the book that will make her famous. It ends six years later, with Alice a young lady of sixteen. Deborah Watling played both parts, but the bulk of the film is weighted toward ten-year-old Alice. Watling, at seventeen, is just too old to be seen as a naive prepubescent girl.

Framed as a story within a story, the film begins and ends with Carroll traveling on a train, where he is accosted by a young woman traveling with her fiancé. The woman fondly recalls the famous author from her childhood, when he used to regale her with stories. But Carroll is ill at ease with the praise, and the reminder of his past sets him off on a reverie. The audience travels back with him to when he first became friends with Alice Liddell.

The film does a good job of showing how offhanded remarks and conversations spark Carroll's imagination, and eventually end up as material for the Alice books. For instance, Carroll is shown talking with a gardener who is pruning a white rose bush. The gardener's young apprentice makes a fanciful remark about painting the roses red. No more is said, but Carroll clearly is taken with the idea and we are led to assume that is how he got the idea for the playing cards painting the rosebush in *Alice's Adventures in Wonderland*.

Alice ran for a little more than an hour on the BBC, on October 13, 1965. Potter later revisited the script and adapted it for the big screen. He kept the flashbacks to when Carroll was first composing his story, but instead of Carroll reminiscing about his past, it is Alice, an octogenarian, who experiences her childhood again. (For an overview of the movie, see *Dreamchild*, page 71.)

Today, Deborah Watling is better known for her 1967–68 role as Victoria Waterfield in the BBC series *Doctor Who.*

In Miller's production, the Mad Tea Party guests are dressed as proper Victorians. Their behavior is what marks them as odd, not their appearance.

Alice in Wonderland

BBC. Directed by Jonathan Miller. 1966.

The BBC's original broadcast of Jonathan Miller's *Alice in Wonderland* at 9:05 p.m. on December 28, 1966, caused an uproar. Media critics were outraged that a book written for the amusement of children had been adapted into a production meant solely for adults and was being shown at such a late hour. What's more, instead of dressing Carroll's familiar and beloved characters in animal costumes and as playing cards, Miller chose to garb all his actors in Victorian dress. Miller, for his part, was unapologetic. The former member of *Beyond the Fringe*, a satiric British revue, stated, "It is a film *about* children, not explicitly *for* them." As for his decision to dispense with traditional costumes in favor of period clothes, he said, "It's much better to simplify, always, rather than elaborate. Movies shouldn't be limited to spectacle; they do the simple things so much better. They should try to present real life in the simplest way possible, and be as unpretentious as possible."

Miller's version stresses the psychological underpinnings of Carroll's work. It shows a young girl on the cusp of entering adult society and being baffled by what she observes. Filmed in black-and-white, and directed in a leisurely, even somnolent style, the film opens and ends with Alice reciting stanzas from Wordsworth's ode "Intimations of Immortality from Recollections of Early Childhood," which expresses the poet's belief that only in childhood can the world appear to be "apparell'd in celestial light." Alice is coming to the end of her childhood and already she is melancholy for its loss.

According to Miller's own writings, rather than sticking with the "slavish replicas of rabbit-headed men and courtiers dressed like playing cards," he chose to go in a different direction and to "find the visual details appropriate to a Victorian dream." Therefore, Alice, played by a then-unknown actress, thirteen-year-old Anne-Marie Mallik, follows not the White Rabbit but a gentleman (Wilfrid Brambell) with a walking stick through the woods and into a deserted nineteenth-century building (in reality, the abandoned military hospital in Netley, England, which was torn down not long after the film finished shooting). The Caucus Race is made up of a group of Victorian aristocrats who bore Alice with their aimless chatter. The Caterpillar (played by Sir Michael Redgrave) doesn't perch on a mushroom with his hookah but rather sits at a desk, fussing over an architectural model and interrogating Alice, like a schoolmaster, about her identity.

The rest of the cast is, like Redgrave, a veritable who's who of British acting royalty, including Sir John Gielgud (the Mock Turtle), Peter Sellers (the King of Hearts), and Leo McKern (a truly ugly Duchess). Peter Cook, Miller's cast mate in *Beyond the Fringe*, gives a singular performance as the Hatter, interpreting the character as a soft-spoken, gentle lunatic rather than the customary antic madman viewers are used to seeing.

Throughout her ordeals, Alice remains nonplussed and disengaged, frequently not even bothering to look at what is going on around her. Her dialogue is often delivered in a voice-over, which adds to the film's dreamlike quality. With her wild mass of unruly hair, she appears closer to Carroll's idea of Alice, whose illustrations of her resemble a pre-Raphaelite young lady (as if to play up their likeness, when the film ends, it is his sketches from the original manuscript that we see).

Adding to the dreamlike atmosphere is the haunting, almost psychedelic music of Ravi Shankar, the Indian sitar master, who both scored and performed in the film. Miller said the lulling sound of the sitar was intended to invoke insects buzzing, which is indeed what Alice hears as she drifts off to sleep on the riverbank.

Broadcast in the centenary year of the publication of *Alice's Adventures in Wonderland*, Miller's production illustrates how a classic can be endlessly interpreted and reimagined. By not following in the well-trod footsteps of previous adapters, he created a fresh version that focuses on the end of childhood and the onset of adulthood. As Miller pointed out, "Once you take the animal heads off, you begin to see what it's all about. A small child, surrounded by hurrying, worried people, thinking 'Is that what being grown up is like?'"

Alice Through the Looking-Glass

NBC. Directed by Alan Handley. 1966.

Most adaptations of Lewis Carroll's Alice books focus on *Alice's Adventures in Wonderland* and give short shrift to *Through the Looking-Glass*. This NBC musical production, which aired on November 6, 1966, devotes itself solely to the latter work, even if at one point Alice comes upon a mysterious bottle that says, "Drink Me." Rather than obey, she puts the potion back down, saying, "Oh, no, I've read all about that." The teleplay, written by Albert Simmons, takes more than a few liberties with Carroll's original. While Alice does commit to wanting to be a queen, in this version she must also help defeat the kingdom from the Jabberwock, a fearsome creature played by Jack Palance, decked out from head to toe in one of Bob Mackie's costumes. New characters were added as well, such as Lester the Jester (played by Roy Castle), Alice's protector and companion in this fantastical world. Also making a bizarre appearance midway through the ninety-minute production are three witches from folklore: Snow White's evil stepmother, the witch from Sleeping Beauty, and the crone from Hansel and Gretel.

At twenty years of age, Judi Rolin is much too old to be playing Alice. Although full of pep and enthusiasm, she is too self-assured to play a young child. Rolin does have a strong and commanding singing voice, though, and her songs are impressive. As Alice wanders through Looking-Glass land, periodically running into—and fleeing from—the Jabberwock, she meets the residents of the kingdom, many played by well-known stars from the 1960s. Agnes Moorehead—familiar as Samantha's mother, Endora, on *Bewitched*—plays the Red Queen. Nanette Fabray and Ricardo Montalban are the White Queen and King. Jimmy Durante, sitting on a high wall in a yellow coat and spats, shines as Humpty Dumpty. And the Smothers Brothers are well cast as Tweedledum and Tweedledee.

The songs, with lyrics by Elsie Simmons and music by Mark "Moose" Charlap of *Peter Pan* fame, are catchy. Among the more memorable numbers are "There Are Two Sides to Everything," "I Wasn't Meant to Be Queen," and "Some Summer Day."

While more a variety show than a true adaptation of Carroll's second book, the production holds its own, even if it is corny at times and shows its age with occasional sexist dialogue. The show made history of a sort when it won the first Emmy for costume design, awarded to Ray Aghayan and Bob Mackie.

Right: In this black-and-white publicity still, Jimmy Durante (Humpty Dumpty) hams it up with Judi Rolin (Alice).

The costume design for the Red Queen, as played by Judy Parfitt (right), was closely modeled on Tenniel's drawing (above).

Alice Through the Looking-Glass

BBC. Directed by James MacTaggart. 1973.

In this BBC adaptation of Carroll's sequel, Alice was played by eleven-year-old Sarah Sutton, who in the following decade would go on to play Nyssa in *Doctor Who*. Sutton gives a natural and believable performance of a young girl who stumbles into a strange, topsy-turvy land. The other members of the cast put in equally strong performances, most notably Brenda Bruce as the White Queen and Judy Parfitt as the Red Queen. Freddie Jones, a British character actor, plays an amusingly droll Humpty Dumpty, who both charms and aggravates Alice with his questions.

The production is remarkably faithful to Carroll's book, even down to minor details. During the scene in which Alice takes a railroad journey, she is dressed in a porkpie hat and cloak, exactly as she's portrayed in Tenniel's drawing. A few incidents are, however, excluded, such as when Alice meets the fawn in the forest, and some of the poems, including the "The Walrus and the Carpenter," are noticeably trimmed.

Director James MacTaggart did an admirable job of creating a credible adaptation of Carroll's second Alice story. And if the production values aren't high to modern eyes, they aren't terrible either. MacTaggart did his best with the technology available to him. In the 1970s, the development of special effects like color keying, which allowed actors to be electronically placed against a variety of illustrated backdrops, meant that directors could do away with physical scenery. In *Alice Through the Looking-Glass*, MacTaggart based his backdrops on Tenniel's drawings and then superimposed Alice and the eccentric inhabitants of Looking-Glass Land against them. A critic writing for the *Stage and Television Today* gave MacTaggart full marks for his embrace of the new technology, declaring that the "esoteric settings and production techniques were employed not for their own sake, but to create an atmosphere of 'dreamlike fantasy,' enabling Alice to interact with a variety of imaginary characters."

Alice in Wonderland

CBS. Irwin Allen Productions. Directed by Harry Harris. 1985.

A live-action television extravaganza broadcast on CBS in December of 1985, *Alice in Wonderland* was shown on two consecutive nights. The first half of the production is taken up with *Alice's Adventures in Wonderland* and the second part with *Through the Looking-Glass*. Unusual for most adaptations, Harris' version features an Alice who is a bona fide child. Natalie Gregory, a nine-year-old American actress, gives an energetic performance, playing Alice with considerable assurance and aplomb. When this Alice lands in Wonderland she's not content to wander around seeing the fantastic sights. In his screenplay, Paul Zindel has Alice wanting to find her way back home, much like Dorothy Gale does when she finds herself in Oz.

Unlike other Alices—including the original—who want to venture into the garden because it is so beautiful, the only reason this production's Alice enters it is to find her way back to her family. Her homesickness persists throughout both parts; no sooner has she escaped from the Knave's trial and landed home than she discovers she is not quite back—she's landed on the other side of the looking-glass. Peering through the mirror, she can see her cat, Dinah, and her parents preparing for an evening out, but she can't make herself be seen or heard. When she reads the poem "Jabberwocky" from a book and conjures up the fearsome beast, it pursues her, apparently as a visualization of her fear she must conquer before she is allowed home.

Wonderland and the Looking-Glass worlds are both populated with Carroll's characters, including some rarely seen in adaptations, such as the Lion and the Unicorn from Carroll's second book. A bit more confusingly, the production also includes animals not included in either of the two books. Soon after Alice meets a lost fawn in the woods (which does take place in *Through the Looking-Glass*), she comes across a baby goat and then a baby chimp. She instructs each animal to go back to its mother before continuing on her way.

The television special boasts an all-star cast, and indeed most of the names are instantly recognizable. Red Buttons (the White Rabbit), Sammy Davis Jr. (the Caterpillar), Martha Raye (the Duchess), Imogene Coca (the Cook), and Carol Channing (the White Queen) are but a few examples. Even Ringo Starr makes an appearance as a very believable—and mournful—Mock Turtle.

Filmed at MGM Studios on a set near where *The Wizard of Oz* was shot, the fourteen-million-dollar, star-studded production also includes music and dance numbers that are mostly forgettable. Despite the scariness of the Jabberwock, the miniseries was intended to be entertaining fare for the whole family.

Below: Wearing an orange-hued dress instead of the traditional blue and a blond wig to hide her dark hair, Natalie Gregory won the part of Alice after a talent hunt that stretched to England and France. Here, she's chatting with the Caterpillar, played by Sammy Davis, Jr.

Alice in Wonderland

BBC. Directed by Barry Letts. 1986.

A straightforward adaptation aimed squarely at young viewers, this BBC production doesn't deviate much from Carroll's classic, staying faithful to the author's dialogue and including most scenes from the book. And unlike many adaptations, this version doesn't include any scenes or characters from *Through the Looking-Glass*. That said, there is not much else to commend this retelling.

Aired in four episodes, each running for approximately thirty minutes, the production is plodding at times, without a sense of whimsy. The overall look reveals the show's low budget. When Alice first enters the garden, the scenery is obviously a painted backdrop and any magical feeling that should accompany the scene is lost. Perhaps the biggest misstep, though, is in the casting. Kate Dorning, as Alice, is all wide-eyed innocence, yet the actress is clearly in her twenties, and when the camera zooms in for a close-up, this fact is made all the more obvious.

Each episode begins and ends with a scene of Lewis Carroll telling his story to the three Liddell sisters on that fateful summer day. For once, Carroll (David Leonard) is properly shown as a vibrant young man and not—as in so many other productions—as a middle-aged, stuttering don. (Carroll was only thirty when he first created the story of *Alice's Adventures in Wonderland*.) However, in these sepia-toned scenes, the similarity in age between the actors who play Alice and Carroll is difficult to ignore.

Directed by Barry Letts of *Doctor Who* fame, the production features quite a few performers from that series (though they are not easily recognizable under heavy makeup), including Elisabeth Sladen (the Dormouse), Brian Miller (the Gryphon), Roy Skelton (the Mock Turtle), and Michael Wisher (the Cheshire Cat).

Adventures in Wonderland

Disney Channel. 1992–1995.

Shown on the Disney Channel from 1992 to 1995, this live-action television series portrays Alice as a contemporary child able to access Wonderland through her bedroom mirror. Once in Wonderland, she interacts with the residents there (a combination of characters from *Alice's Adventures in Wonderland* and *Through the Looking-Glass*), fixing their problems and mediating their spats. Often, the resolution of the Wonderland kerfuffles helps Alice solve her own problems back home. Child actress Elisabeth Harnois is an energetic Alice, singing and dancing her way through various numbers. The main Wonderland characters include the Red Queen (Armelia McQueen), the White Rabbit (Patrick Richwood), the Mad Hatter (John Robert Hoffman), the March Hare (Reece Holland), Tweedledee (Harry Waters Jr.) and Tweedledum (Robert Barry Fleming), the Caterpillar (Wesley Mann), the Cheshire Cat (puppet), and the Dormouse (puppet). Teri Garr makes occasional appearances as the Duchess. Throughout its 100-episode-run, the show won a handful of Emmys, including ones for makeup, writing, and directing.

For his part as the White Rabbit, actor Patrick Richwood (far right) was required to rollerblade.

Alice Through the Looking-Glass

BBC. Directed by John Henderson. 1998.

In this BBC television production, Alice (Kate Beckinsale) is a mother reading *Through the Looking-Glass* to her blond-haired daughter. You might reasonably expect the young girl, a child about eight years old, to be transported through the mirror, but that never happens; instead, it is the mother who sails through the glass. Even more curious—and never explained—is why when she reaches the other side, she keeps referring to herself as a seven-year-old, when she is obviously not. Adding to the confusion, Beckinsale was pregnant at the time of the filming and at certain camera angles her condition is obvious. In spite of a few of these obstacles, Beckinsale is a plucky Alice who navigates the absurd world she finds herself in with the right mixture of charm and bravado.

Overall the production is a faithful and well-done version of Carroll's second book. Once in this strange land, Alice sets out across a landscaped chessboard to become a queen. Along the way, she meets most of the characters found in the original story. Viewers familiar with British actors will recognize Geoffrey Palmer as the White King and Penelope Wilton as his wife. Comedian and actor Steve Coogan plays the Gnat in the train scene, and Ian Holm is the gallant but clumsy White Knight. In an interesting aside, Holm was knighted the same year he played the part.

The production stands out from other adaptations for including the "Wasp in the Wig," a chapter from *Through the Looking-Glass* that Carroll had intended to use but was talked out of by Tenniel, who convinced the author that the episode wasn't interesting enough. Shakespearian actor Ian Richardson plays the yellow-wigged insect.

Alice in Wonderland

NBC. Directed by Nick Willing. 1999.

Director Nick Willing's version of *Alice in Wonderland* is bracketed with a storyline not found in Carroll's books. Willing begins his three-hour primetime special, first aired on NBC on February 28, 1999, with a scene showing Alice, played by thirteen-year-old Tina Majorino, nervously preparing for a recital at her parents' garden party. Stricken with a bad case of stage fright, Alice runs away at the last moment to take refuge on the estate grounds under the boughs of an apple tree. There, she drifts off to sleep and soon is following the White Rabbit off to Wonderland.

The story then proceeds mostly as Carroll depicted. The movie covers nearly all of *Alice's Adventures in Wonderland*, as well as including some of the highlights of *Through the Looking-Glass*, such as the scenes where Alice meets the talking flowers and the White Knight. Unlike Carroll's books, though, the film comes with a tidy moral, one that is summed up when Alice encounters the White Knight in the forest. When Alice confesses her nervousness about performing, he advises her "to get back on the horse" and "Just be brave!" Other characters she meets offer helpful advice as well. The Mock Turtle encourages Alice to come out of her shell and coaxes her into singing "Turtle Soup."

In the movie's penultimate scene, Alice stands up to the Queen of Hearts and the court, and, in effect, "performs" in front of them. The White Rabbit remarks on her newfound confidence and declares, "…you don't need us anymore." The dream world disappears and Alice is back under the apple tree. Needless to say, she is able to sing at the garden party, though the song she warbles is "The Lobster Quadrille," taught to her by the Mock Turtle back in Wonderland.

Willing professed to love the book and said he "approached it reverently." Still, when he adapted the book for the screen, he felt it needed to be altered:

"The main thing I insisted on is that Alice is asked to sing a song and is scared. The reason I did that is I felt the book is a collection of anecdotes, sketches written at different times and then cobbled together in a book. It is not written as a story with a beginning, middle, and end. And our modern movie sensibility has to have an emotional pull for us to stay with a character."

The Hallmark television special with its mix of live action and puppetry is made up of an all-star cast. Whoopi Goldberg lends her wide-mouth grin to the Cheshire Cat; Gene Wilder hams it up as the mournful Mock Turtle; and Ben Kingsley is the mystical Caterpillar. Two especially notable performances belong to Martin Short as the Hatter and to Miranda Richardson as the Queen of Hearts. Short's Hatter is a masterful blend of zaniness and logic, and watching his portrayal is like seeing Tenniel's illustrations come to life. Richardson uses her considerable acting talents to transform the Queen of Hearts into a truly mad and capricious character. With her bright-red pouty lips, the spoiled queen must always get her way.

Martin Short as the Hatter in Willing's 1999 *Alice in Wonderland*.

Jim Henson's Creature Shop designed the puppets, including the White Rabbit, the Cheshire Cat, the Gryphon, the March Hare, the Dormouse, the Duchess' baby, the croquet-stick flamingoes, and the guinea pig jurors. The film's visual look and special effects are its highlights, and it ended up winning four Emmys for costume design, makeup, music composition, and visual effects.

While acknowledging that the film included many fine renditions of individual scenes, many critics felt that the production suffered from slow pacing. A review in *Variety* summed it up best:

"At times wildly entertaining and even poignant, 'Alice' ultimately winds up being a trifle too much—too lengthy, too broad, too unwieldy. Even the impressive visual elements are so multitudinous as to almost detract from any overall magical effect. Indeed, for all of its production's tricks, Alice's journey through Wonderland suffers passages of sheer tedium."

An apprehensive Alice (Tina Majorino) is escorted to see the Queen of Hearts.

Alice

Syfy. Written and directed by Nick Willing. 2009.

Ten years after Nick Willing directed an adaptation of *Alice in Wonderland* for NBC (see page 92), he was inspired to try his hand again at interpreting Carroll's classic. Willing wasn't interested in just translating the book into film though. This time around he wanted to "reimagine" Wonderland and bring it 150 years into the future. Willing had already tried something similar with another fantasy-based children's classic. In 2007, he freely adapted *The Wizard of Oz* into *The Tin Man*. The miniseries played on Syfy and did well in the ratings, garnering critical acclaim.

The premise behind the *Alice* miniseries is that over the years Wonderland has become a high-tech empire that depends on "oysters"—abducted humans imported from our world—whose emotions are stolen from them while, sedated, they play games in a futuristic casino. The extracted emotions, such as desire, ecstasy, and awe, are then dispensed to the masses to keep them addicted and compliant.

Alice (Caterina Scorsone) stumbles into this alternate universe (falling through a large mirror, or looking-glass, set against a building wall in a dark alley) while chasing after a man called White Rabbit who, with his minions, has abducted her new boyfriend, Jack Chase (Philip Winchester).

As Alice, Caterina Scorsone (above) must match wits with the crafty Queen of Hearts (Kathy Bates, left).

Once in Wonderland, Alice, a twenty-something martial arts instructor, attempts to search for Jack. She's helped by Hatter (Andrew-Lee Potts), a street-smart local who may or may not be trustworthy. As the pair navigate the crumbling cityscape, they come across familiar Wonderland characters, as reimagined by Willing. The Queen of Hearts, played to the autocratic hilt by Kathy Bates, rules the land, and while not every order out of her mouth is "Off with their heads," the phrase does crop up once or twice. And, as in Carroll's original, her slavish husband (Colm Meaney), usually rescinds the execution once her back is turned. Tweedledee and Tweedledum are the Queen's creepy torturers, and they do a superb job of interrogating Alice in the Truth Room after she is inevitably captured. The Queen's assassin, the March Hare, is a cyborg; he sports the porcelain head of a cookie jar in the shape of a rabbit. Fighting against the Queen are the members of the resistance, led by a mysterious man called Caterpillar (Harry Dean Stanton).

Several eye-opening revelations await Alice. First, she learns that Jack Chase is none other than Jack Heart, the Queen's royal son. Still reeling from that news, she discovers that Jack is in fact working for the resistance and that he brought her to Wonderland in the hope that she can awaken memories in Carpenter (Timothy Webber), a scientist who devises and administers the emotions that keep Wonderland's royal subjects under the Queen's control. Carpenter, you see, is Alice's long-lost father.

Aired on Syfy and Canadian cable television a year before Tim Burton's *Alice in Wonderland* (see page 73) was released, the miniseries shares many of the film's themes. Both do away with Carroll's episodic series of vignettes and instead impose a quest plot on the story. Alice, no longer a child, has an involved backstory, which she must overcome in order to lead her own life. In Burton's version, she must develop the courage to turn down a suitor; in Willing's she has to come to terms with her father's disappearance and her problems with commitment. Finally, in both productions, Alice and the Hatter pair up to fight injustices together.

While the ratings for *Alice* were strong, critical reception for the two-part miniseries was mixed, with some reviewers complaining that the pacing dragged, especially in the beginning. Others appreciated Willing's creativity and his readiness to scramble things up instead of treating Carroll's works as sacred texts. As David Hinckley wrote in his review for the *Daily News*: "Some purists will scowl at the liberties Willing has taken with Carroll's Alice. But it was written as fancy, a vehicle to engage the imagination while it amuses and entertains, and this version remains true to that mission."

Once Upon a Time in Wonderland
ABC Studios. Created by Edward Kitsis, Adam Horowitz, Zack Estrin, and Jane Espenson. 2013.

ABC's series, which premiered in October 2013, was a spinoff of *Once Upon a Time*, a show that throws together fairy-tale characters from a number of sources—Snow White, Peter Pan, and Rumplestiltskin, to name a few—to see how they play together (usually not very nicely). Using a similar approach, *Once Upon a Time in Wonderland* takes Carroll's Alice and the Wonderland setting, and grafts it with characters from Disney's *Aladdin*.

Through a number of flashbacks, the series' pilot episode explains how the two worlds have collided. After young Alice (Sophie Lowe) returns from Wonderland, her father (Shaun Smyth), who had thought her dead, refuses to believe her strange story of disappearing cats and talking rabbits. In the ensuing years, Alice returns several times to Wonderland, seeking proof that will convince her father. On one such trip, now a young woman, she falls in love with Cyrus (Peter Gadiot), a genie she meets when she scrambles into his bottle to escape the Queen's henchmen. How did the genie end up in Wonderland? Long ago he flew through a Middle-Eastern portal to escape the evil Jafar (Naveen Andrews).

Alice stays in Wonderland with Cyrus until they have a run-in with the Red Queen (Emma Rigby), which ends with Cyrus plunging off a cliff and into the boiling sea. Alice, believing her love to be dead, returns once again to her Victorian world, brokenhearted, and is institutionalized by her father. At the asylum, on the verge of undergoing some kind of lobotomy, Alice is sprung by the Knave of Hearts (Michael Socha), who informs her that Cyrus may still be alive.

Once back in Wonderland, Alice, with the reluctant help of the Knave of Hearts, sets out to track down Cyrus. In subsequent episodes, Alice and Cyrus, reunited, go up against an assortment of villains and receive help from those sympathetic to their cause. Some, such as the White Rabbit, the Caterpillar, the Cheshire Cat, and the Bandersnatch, will be familiar to fans of Carroll's books; others, such as Grendel, a monster from the Anglo-Saxon medieval epic poem *Beowulf*, may not be.

Reviews of the series were mostly positive. The series production values received high marks, and most critics agreed that Australian actress Sophia Lowe made a compelling and appealing Alice. Michael Socha as the Knave of Hearts and Naveen Andrews as Jafar were singled out for their performances as well. David Wiegand, writing for the *San Francisco Chronicle*, summed up the series: "The plot is a little overstuffed, but the special effects, crisp direction, and high-octane performances keep us interested enough to follow Alice down the rabbit hole." Despite the positive reviews though, the series did not attain a high enough viewership and was subsequently cancelled in 2014.

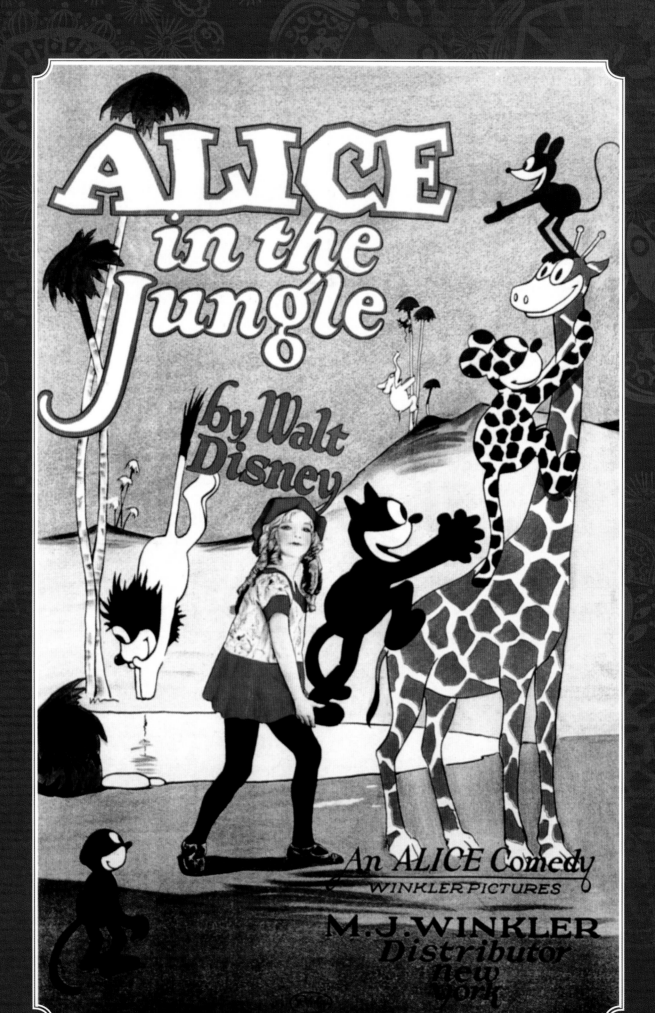

CHAPTER 6
Animated Alice

"The animation of Alice in Wonderland *presented the most formidable problems we have ever faced in translating a literary classic into the cartoon medium."*

—Walt Disney from the article "How I Cartooned 'Alice'"

As Walt Disney mentions in the above quote, animators face unique challenges when adapting Carroll's Alice books. In addition to all the usual problems that would be involved in creating any movie version of Alice, such as finding a suspenseful narrative in Carroll's episodic tale, animators also have to create the look and movements of the characters from scratch, either by drawing them or through puppetry. As Disney succinctly stated in an article he wrote, titled "How I Cartooned 'Alice'": "It is not easy technically, to turn book illustrations into animated cartoons." Yet a fair number of animators have done just that. Beginning with Disney himself, who in 1923 set a live-action Alice in the middle of a cartoon Wonderland, and continuing to the present, when Matt Groening inserts sly references to *Alice in Wonderland* in his hit series *The Simpsons*, animators have struggled to wrestle Alice and her story to the drawing board.

Left: A promotional poster for Walt Disney's *Alice in the Jungle* released in 1925. Virginia Davis starred as Alice.
Right: A sketch of Alice by artist Zsófia Szabó.

Alice's Wonderland

Laugh-O-Gram Films. Directed by Walt Disney. 1923.

Long before Disney's full-length *Alice in Wonderland* hit theaters in 1951, Walt Disney directed this twelve-and-a-half-minute animated short that was never released commercially. The black-and-white silent film combines live action with animation. Although the short has nothing much in common with Lewis Carroll's classic, except the similar title and the conceit of a child visiting a fantastical land, it does demonstrate Disney's interest in the Alice books early in his career.

In the one-reel short, Alice, played by four-year-old curlylocks Virginia Davis, visits Disney's Kansas City Laugh-O-Gram studio to see how cartoons are made. A young Walt Disney shows her around, and she watches in delight as animated animals magically perform for her on a drawing board. That night, Alice dreams she is in Cartoonland, where she is feted with a grand parade. Later, as she dances for her new friends, four lions escape from the zoo and chase her, forcing her to jump off a cliff. She free falls (much like the original Alice's tumble down the rabbit hole), eventually waking up safe in her bed.

In the end, the film was never released in theaters. Laugh-O-Gram Studio filed for bankruptcy shortly after the film was completed. But that's not to say Disney wasted his time. He showed *Alice's Wonderland* to cartoon distributors, and one of them, Margaret J. Winkler, whose franchises included Felix the Cat, signed him and his brother Roy to a contract that stipulated they create more Alice films. Fifty-six additional *Alice Comedies* were produced between 1923 and 1924, and a new company was founded, one that we know today as the Walt Disney Company.

Virginia Davis starred in thirteen of the fifty-six *Alice Comedies*. She said of working with Disney: "When Walt was directing me he'd say 'Let's pretend.' Then he'd tell me the story of the scene. We had to get it right on the first take because Walt and Roy couldn't afford to buy film for take two."

Betty in Blunderland

Produced by Max Fleischer. Directed by Dave Fleisher. 1934.

Betty Boop, a caricature of a sexy Jazz Age flapper, made her first appearance in the 1930 animated short *Dizzy Dishes* as an anthropomorphic poodle. As the love interest of Bimbo, a dog character in Max Fleischer's Talkartoons series, Betty has her trademark saucer eyes and shapely legs, but she also has ears that flap. By 1931's *Mask-a-Raid*, Betty has shed her canine appearance and is now recognizably human, with large hoop earrings in place of dog ears. It wasn't long before Betty was a hit, with her own fan clubs, comic strip, and radio show. In April 1934, *Betty in Blunderland* was released; almost seven minutes long, the short is based on a combination of *Alice's Adventures in Wonderland* and *Through the Looking-Glass*.

We meet Betty late at night as she assembles an *Alice in Wonderland* jigsaw puzzle (based on Tenniel's original illustrations). Growing tired, Betty places the White Rabbit's head and he springs to life, disappearing through the looking-glass. Betty follows and, once through the mirror, finds herself in front of a subway station. Inside she falls down a shaft. To get through the tiny door, Betty drinks a foaming mug of "Shrink-ola" that looks suspiciously like beer. Immediately she is small. Interestingly, her dress doesn't shrink with her, but a blast of water from a showerhead soon fixes that.

Many familiar characters from Carroll's two books appear, including the Hatter, the Duchess, and Tweedledee and Tweedledum (both of whom bear a striking resemblance to 1930s baseball phenomenon Babe Ruth). As Betty sings a jazzy "How Do You Do" number to the assembled characters, the Jabberwock swoops down and captures her. The other characters come to her rescue, and Betty wakes up in her living room in front of the incomplete puzzle.

Betty in Blunderland was one of the cartoon character's last appearances as a freewheeling single girl. The Production Code, or Hays Code, went into effect in July 1934 and imposed restrictions on what it deemed unacceptable content. Over time, Betty's clothes became modest, her snazzy jewelry disappeared, and even her hair lost some of its curls. Betty Boop morphed into a respectable young woman, one who would never be so carefree as to drink a mug of Shrink-ola or to dally in Blunderland.

Thru the Mirror

Walt Disney Productions. Directed by David Hand. 1936.

Mickey Mouse made his debut in 1928's *Steamboat Willie* and a star was born. The little mouse was featured in hundreds of cartoon shorts, but it was his eighty-third appearance that revealed Disney's continuing fascination with Lewis Carroll's books. Thirteen years after Disney directed Virginia Davis in *Alice in Wonderland* for Laugh-O-Gram, he was reimagining Carroll's fantasy worlds. The short, released by United Artists on May 30, 1936, runs for almost nine minutes and was inspired by Carroll's two books. As in Disney's 1923 *Alice in Wonderland*, Mickey falls asleep and in his dream slips through the looking-glass and into a topsy-turvy version of his house. Although the method for entering the fantasy land—and the short's title—reference Carroll's second Alice book, the cartoon borrows freely from the first book as well. Mickey explores the other side of the mirror and finds that all his household belongings have been anthropomorphized. The chair he falls on protests

and the footstool is a growling dog. When Mickey accepts and eats a walnut from a personified nutcracker, he grows into a giant, hitting his head on the ceiling, only to immediately shrink to the size of a playing card. In his new miniature state, Mickey delights in being small. A mouse version of Fred Astaire, he dances through a wide array of spectacular effects (at one point even performing with a top hat, cane, and a pair of white gloves). *Top Hat* starring Astaire and Ginger Rogers had come out the year before, so Mickey's soft-shoe antics were most likely a tribute. The short ends with Mickey interacting with playing cards, another nod to *Alice in Wonderland*. He dances with the Queen of Hearts, whom the animators depicted as Greta Garbo. Their cavorting arouses the ire of the King of Hearts (a caricature of Charles Laughton, another leading Hollywood star). The King and all the playing cards rush after Mickey, who defends himself as best as he can, at one point turning the fan on his foes to scatter them. The cards, though, continue to chase after him until he escapes back through the mirror and wakes up safe and sound in his own bed.

A young Walt Disney with Mickey Mouse circa 1930.

Alice in Wonderland

Lou Bunin Productions. Directed by Dallas Bower and Lou Bunin. 1949.

Lou Bunin's version of *Alice in Wonderland* sneaked into New York's Mayfair Theater just two days before Walt Disney's animated film premiered at the Criterion. It had to have been a bitter pill for Disney to swallow since his company had sued—and lost—to delay Bunin's live-action-and-puppet film from appearing in the United States, claiming that audiences would be deceived into seeing the wrong film. Bunin's victory, however, was short lived. Critics panned the film. Bosley Crowther of the *New York Times* called it "a nightmare" and so "lacking in humor that it is almost Tolstoyan in mood." He then described the puppets as "ugly" and the sets as "uncomfortably tasteless."

It didn't help that Carol Marsh, the British actress who played Alice, was twenty years old, a bit long in the tooth to play a seven-year-old girl.

The film, which originally was produced and released in France in 1949 but made its first appearance in the United States in 1951, took several years to complete and used stop-motion animation to film the puppets. The tiny puppets, less than seven inches high, were enlarged on film. Bunin, a talented puppeteer and a pioneer in stop-motion animation, also had trouble getting his film seen in England. British censors didn't care for his Queen of Hearts puppet, which they viewed as a cruel caricature of Queen Victoria. Audiences in England didn't get to see the film until 1985. Although the film didn't do well when it was first released, the Museum of Modern Art later restored the film, and it now has a cult following.

Carol Marsh poses with the puppet for the White Rabbit.

Alice in Wonderland

Walt Disney Productions. Directed by Clyde Geronimi, Wilfred Jackson, and Hamilton Luske. 1951.

Throughout his career, Walt Disney kept returning to Lewis Carroll's *Alice's Adventures in Wonderland*, playing with the idea of a feature-length film but never really committing to one. In the early 1920s, he made a live-action/animation short that referenced *Alice's Adventures in Wonderland* (see page 102), and in 1936, he had Mickey Mouse step through the looking-glass and enter a Wonderland-inspired fantasy land (see page 104). But it wasn't until 1951 that his definitive *Alice in Wonderland* came out in theaters. Along the way to its release there were so many bumps in the road that it's a small miracle the film made it into the theaters at all.

Disney had been taken with *Alice's Adventures in Wonderland* since childhood. In a 1946 article in *American Weekly*, he states: "No story in English literature has intrigued me more than Lewis Carroll's *Alice in Wonderland*. It fascinated me the first time I read it as a schoolboy and as soon as I possibly could after I started making animated cartoons, I acquired the film rights to it." Disney bought the rights to the Alice books—and the rights to Tenniel's illustrations—in 1938, right after he finished *Snow White*, his first feature film. Five years earlier, though, he had been toying with the idea of making a full-length feature film with Mary Pickford, the silent screen star. Pickford had proposed the project to Disney, intending to play the live-action role of Alice, while Disney and his band of artists would animate Wonderland and its fantastic characters. The idea, however, was scrapped when Paramount came out with its all-star movie version of Wonderland in 1933 (see page 62).

After Disney purchased the rights in 1938, he put his staff to work to come up with a treatment. Al Perkins, one of the writers, eventually produced an analysis of the book with suggestions of possible ways to animate the story. Other writers were pessimistic. Bob Carr, the onetime head of the story department, complained, "There is no story in the book." He also had his doubts about Alice. "Alice has no character," he stated. "She merely plays the straight man to a cast of screwball comics."

Still, work advanced enough that in 1939, David Hall, a British artist, produced a number of sketches, drawings, and paintings for Wonderland. In November of that year, the studio did a short film to get an idea of how the finished movie would look. Disney was not particularly impressed with the results. "There are certain things in there that I like very much and there are other things in there that I think we should tear right out," he asserted. He suggested letting the project sit; and sit it did for another six years.

Although Hall's treatment had been for full animation, Disney was undecided and at times veered toward a combination of live-action and animation. At one point, he seriously considered Ginger Rogers for the title role. Another time, he toyed with hiring Luana Patten, the young star of *Song of the South*, for the part.

In 1945, during his quest to find a unique treatment for his project, Disney brought in a famous British novelist. Aldous Huxley, best known for his novel *Brave New World*, prepared a synopsis for a film that would combine animation with live action and that was to be called *Alice and the Mysterious Mr. Carroll*. Disney rejected the treatment in short order, famously commenting that he "could only understand every third word" of the script.

Eventually, Disney settled on an all-cartoon feature film and hired Kathryn Beaumont, a preteen English girl, to be the voice of Alice. At first, the studio attempted to draw the animation in a style as close to Tenniel's as possible. But as work progressed, it became clear to all that Tenniel's detailed style of drawing could not be successfully duplicated. So more cartoony Disney-like characters were developed, although they retained Tenniel's overall look. As Walt Disney explained in "How I Cartooned 'Alice'":

Above: Walt Disney at the Dorcester hotel reading his company's adaptation of *Alice In Wonderland* with a model of Donald Duck.

Above: Walt Disney and Kathryn Beaumont (who voiced "Alice" in the 1951 Disney version of *Alice in Wonderland*) looking at artwork from the film.

"For the cartoon medium, the characters virtually had to be born anew, since their behavior would have to be conveyed in movement, rather than with words and pen-and-ink drawings. And yet, I think we have managed to follow Tenniel in such close detail that no one can say our delineations distort the images Carroll and Tenniel worked out together."

The finished movie was based mostly on Carroll's *Alice's Adventures in Wonderland* with a smattering of *Through the Looking-Glass* thrown in. The singing flowers are from the latter book, as are Tweedledee and Tweedledum reciting the poem about the Walrus and the Carpenter. While most of the film adheres closely to Carroll's original story, Disney did deviate

Above: A promotional poster for Walt Disney's 1951 *Alice in Wonderland*.

here and there, usually for reasons of pacing. The entire "Pig and Pepper" chapter is missing, although a 1939 version of the scene still exists. Another deleted scene was one in which Alice meets the dreaded Jabberwock, only to discover the creature to be more comical than fearsome. The Mock Turtle, the Gryphon, and the White Knight were other discarded characters. As he often did in his movies, Disney inserted a new character into the mix, in this case the talking doorknob. According to Disney, the doorknob was invented "in order to avoid a long explanatory monologue at the beginning of the story and to give Alice a foil to talk to." Ever anxious

not to offend Lewis Carroll fans, he was quick to point out that the talking doorknob was approved "by some of the strictest of Alice purists in England."

Despite his adherence to Carroll's classic, Disney couldn't help but sanitize and sweeten Carroll's darker view of society in relation to childhood. Where in the original the Wonderland characters snap and bark at Alice, commanding her to perform and causing her distress, in Disney's version, the collection of oddballs she meets is more zany and goofy than antagonistic. *Alice in Wonderland* becomes wholesome family fare rather than bracing social commentary.

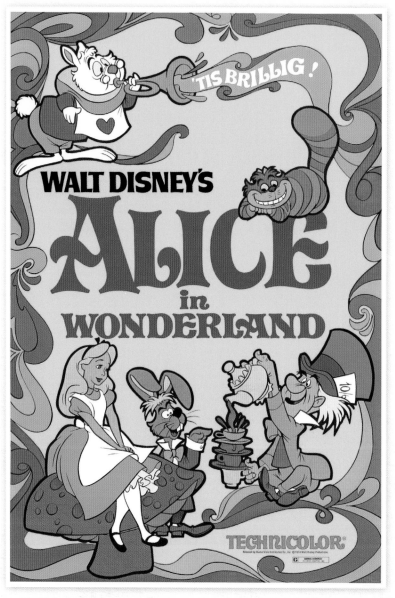

Disney eventually re-released its underachiever in 1974, even going so far as to market it as a "head film." This poster's psychedelic colors emphasize the film's appeal to college students.

The film boasts an unusually long list of songs, the most of any Disney movie of the time. The title song, "Alice in Wonderland," went on to become a jazz standard, performed by many notable musicians, including jazz pianist Dave Brubeck. Some of the songs were based on Carroll's verses; others were the invention of modern songwriters. Arguably the most famous song to emerge from the movie was "The Unbirthday Song," a rollicking feel-good romp of a tune. One of the songs written for *Alice in Wonderland* was repurposed in another Disney film. The melody for "Beyond the Laughing Sky," a ballad Alice sings that is reminiscent of Judy Garland's "Somewhere Over the Rainbow," became "The Second Star to the Right" in *Peter Pan.*

When the film at last reached theaters in the summer of 1951, the critical response was less than enthusiastic. Despite Disney's heavy promotion, the first release didn't earn out its $3 million investment. One of the major critiques was that Disney had bowdlerized a classic, which perhaps wasn't fair, as Disney, although respectful of Carroll's text, had

wanted from the start to bring *Alice in Wonderland* into the twentieth century. In a 1939 meeting, he declared, "There is a spirit behind Carroll's story. It's fantasy, imagination, and screwball logic . . . but it must be funny. To hell with the English audience or the people who love Carroll . . . I'd like to make it more or less a 1940 or 1945 version—right up to date." Nonetheless, a reviewer in the *New Yorker* wrote, "In Mr. Disney's *Alice* there is a blind incapacity to understand that a literary masterwork cannot be improved by the introduction of shiny little tunes, and touches more suited to a flea circus than to a major imaginative effort."

Disney ultimately was dissatisfied with his film as well. Admitting that it was "terribly tough to transfer whimsy to the screen," he viewed the film as "a terrible disappointment." His final assessment was that "the film lacked heart." *Alice in Wonderland* didn't really find its footing until the psychedelic 1960s rolled around. College students flocked to see screenings of it on 16-mm film on campuses across the country, reveling in the hookah-smoking caterpillar, the hallucinatory mushroom, and the trippy escapades.

Artist Ron Embleton's *Walrus and the Carpenter.*

Alice in Wonderland (or What's a Nice Girl Like You Doing in a Place Like This?)

Hanna-Barbera Productions. Directed by Alex Lovy. 1966.

This prime-time musical spoof of Carroll's classic books aired on ABC on March 30, 1966. Instead of going down a rabbit hole or through the looking-glass to get to Wonderland, this Alice—a suburban teen—goes through the television set in pursuit of her dog, Fluff. Once in Wonderland, Alice (voiced by Janet Waldo, who also did Judy Jetson in *The Jetsons* and Josie McCoy in *Josie and the Pussycats*) meets a zany cast of characters, many voiced by well-known actors and celebrities. Sammy Davis Jr. lends his vocal chords to the Cheshire Cat. A cool beatnik with a beard and beret, the Cheshire Cat sings the show's theme song, "What's a Nice Girl Like You Doing in a Place Like This?" Lyrics such as "Oh, I've got a feeling, you won't like it here. The potato chips are soggy and they water the beer" clue in viewers that this isn't typical kiddie fare. The song was a hit and even made the Top Ten Billboard list. Lee Adams and

Charles Strouse of *Bye Bye Birdie* fame were responsible for all the movie's songs.

Other famous actors include Harvey Korman (the Hatter), Zsa Zsa Gabor (the Queen of Hearts), and the comedian Bill Dana (the White Knight). In her final appearance, the gossip columnist Hedda Hopper turns up as a version of herself at the Mad Tea Party to show off a collection of wacky hats. Produced by Hanna-Barbera, the special even brought in animated characters from its Saturday morning lineup—Fred Flintstone and Barney Rubble make an appearance as a two-headed caterpillar that performs a vaudeville act for Alice, complete with straw hats and canes.

The good-natured script, written by Bill Dana, is heavy on puns and sight gags. When Alice first arrives in Wonderland, a weighty volume opens, and imprinted inside is an endorsement by Lewis Carroll: "This place is all right in my book." Other inside jokes include Humphrey Dumpty (in a takeoff of Humphrey Bogart) doing time in prison for being a bad egg. Alice is reunited with Fluff, and with the help of some Wonderland characters, they escape the clutches of the King and Queen of Hearts and return to the safety of modern-day suburbia.

The Care Bears Adventure in Wonderland

Directed by Raymond Jafelice. 1987.

The brainchild of the American Greetings card company, the Care Bears dominated the toy market and Saturday morning television throughout the mid-1980s. The animated bears also featured in three animated films during the decade, the last of which takes the plush animals to Wonderland. Lewis Carroll would have difficulty recognizing his characters in the mishmash fantasyland that is re-created in the movie. For starters, few actual Wonderland characters appear. The White Rabbit, the Cheshire Cat, the Mad Hatter, and the Jabberwock (from *Through the Looking-Glass*)

have substantial parts, and flamingoes and a traffic-cop Caterpillar put in appearances, but missing are the Duchess, the March Hare, the Mock Turtle, and a host of others. The Queen of Hearts has an active role—except she's one of the good guys. The film's villain is the Wizard of Wonderland, a power-hungry individual intent on stealing the throne from the Princess, who is soon to be crowned. While the Wizard has no match in Carroll's original stories, his minions are Dee and Dum, two piggish creatures modeled on Tweedledee and Tweedledum.

The Care Bears find themselves in Wonderland thanks to the White Rabbit. He is looking for the Princess, whom the Wizard has kidnapped and placed in the care of the Jabberwock. The Care Bears lead the White Rabbit to Alice, an ordinary girl with a cat

As in the 1951 Disney animated feature, the Cheshire Cat is portrayed in psychedelic colors.

The Care Bears Adventures in Wonderland, the third Care Bear movie to be produced, was also the last.

named Dinah who bears a remarkable resemblance to the princess. A plan is hatched to bring Alice to Wonderland to double for the kidnapped Princess until she can be rescued. In Wonderland, Alice, who suffers from low self-esteem, is buoyed by the Care Bears' exhortations that she is indeed special, and gains confidence as she overcomes the obstacles that the Wizard throws at her.

While the pastel-hued animation takes frequent short cuts—only certain parts of a character's body move at times and the scenery is static—the fast-paced action helps keep you from noticing it. Some of the songs are genuinely inventive and capture some of Carroll's sense

of play. The Mad Hatter sings a rousing "Mad About Hats," as he flings headwear on and off his bald dome; likewise, the Cheshire Cat is portrayed as a hip-hop rapper with attitude.

The animated film, which was released by Cineplex Odeon Films on August 7, 1987, received mixed reviews. Most critics agreed that the production would keep children entertained but opined that adults would find few surprises. Hal Hinson of the *Washington Post* summed it up best when he likened watching the movie to "being pelted mercilessly for seventy-five minutes with Lucky Charms."

Alice (Original title: Něco z Alenky)

Written and directed by Jan Švankmajer. 1988.

As the opening credits of this Czech film scroll down the screen, Alice, in a live-action role played by Kristýna Kohoutová, announces to the audience, "Now you will see a film. Made for children. Perhaps." Or perhaps not. Jan Švankmajer's surreal and violent 1998 film, a combination of live action and stop-motion animation, is pretty much guaranteed to give a child of any age nightmares.

Švankmajer, a Czech animator, imbued his first feature-length film with a sense of menace and foreboding. Long influenced by Carroll's classic, he chose to focus on the dream aspect of the novel rather than on its wordplay or its odd collection of characters. In an interview, he opined that other adaptations have presented the story as a fairy tale with an underlying moral; whereas a dream "as an expression of our

unconscious, uncompromisingly pursues the realization of our most secret wishes without considering rational and moral inhibitions, because it is driven by the principle of pleasure." He goes on to state unequivocally, "My *Alice* is a realized dream."

The film loosely follows the book's plot. After the opening credits, Alice is in a room, an unfriendly looking place littered with an assortment of odd objects, many of which later make an appearance in Wonderland. Under a glass display case, a taxidermy white rabbit begins to stir, coming to life. The rabbit pulls out a drawer from the floor of the case and dons a suit he finds inside. Also in the drawer is a large pair of scissors, which he uses to smash his way out of the case. He checks his pocket watch and takes off, leaking sawdust. Alice follows, chasing him through a field. In the middle of the desolate landscape stands a wooden desk. The rabbit disappears through its drawer—no ordinary rabbit hole in this film—and again Alice pursues him.

Instead of tumbling, an elevator takes her down below. Wonderland in this avant-garde film is not quite like any other. A collection of cramped rooms, each harboring a disturbing or frightening tableau, it is both claustrophobic and overwhelming. Not all of the characters from Carroll's Wonderland appear, though the Caterpillar (a wormlike sock with glass eyes and dentures), the members of the Mad Tea Party, and the King and Queen of Hearts all show up.

The White Rabbit takes on many of the roles, and is indeed a malevolent force throughout the film. Instead of the Cook and the Duchess, it is he who tends to the squalling baby, and when Alice attempts to enter the doll-size house, it is he who throws plates and cookware at her. In another room, Alice stumbles upon the Mad Tea Party, where she finds the Hatter, a marionette, and the March Hare (a wind-up toy playing cards). The White Rabbit interrupts their fun, dashing in with his scissors and cutting off their heads. Unconcerned, the pair switch heads and continue with their game.

For a change, the child who plays Alice is of the appropriate age. Kristýna Kohoutová, the only actor in the production, looks to be around seven years old, precisely the age Carroll specified. Blond and wide-eyed, she makes a credible Alice. It is she who narrates the film, speaking the other characters' parts as well as her own. After reciting a character's lines, the camera zooms in for a close-up of her mouth as she adds a tag line, such as "said the White Rabbit" or "cried the Queen."

The film is sparse with both dialogue and music. Most of the time the audience hears heightened sound effects of drawers squeaking open or plates crashing or papers rustling. When combined with the deliberately jerky movements of the stop-motion animation, this serves to create an eerie and creepy atmosphere.

Released in 1988, the film with its bizarre imagery and underlying theme of unsettling terror has gone on to become a cult favorite. Perhaps, then, it is not much of a surprise to learn that Jan Švankmajer's films have been a major influence on the director of the latest *Alice in Wonderland* film, Tim Burton (see page 73).

The White Rabbit puppet used in the film was an actual rabbit that had been taxidermied.

In one surreal scene, a rodent prepares to cook its dinner on the head of Alice (Kristýna Kohoutová).

The Simpsons

Surprisingly, the Fox network's animated comedy series *The Simpsons* has never tackled *Alice in Wonderland* head on, even though the show is famous for its parodies on popular culture. In the long-running show's seventh season (1995–1996), one episode did highlight two Wonderland characters in a brief scene. In "Summer of 4 Ft. 2," Lisa Simpson is feeling especially unpopular when none of her schoolmates sign her yearbook. When the Simpson family vacations at a beach community, Lisa is determined to start afresh and be one of the cool kids. As she passes the local library, she is tempted to go inside. Instead, she daydreams that various literary characters from books have come to life. In one of the dream sequences, Alice and the Hatter appear. Alice is in the middle of inviting Lisa to join their tea party when she cries out, "Don't do it, Lisa. It's a trick!" The Hatter then grabs Alice and holds a gun to her head as Alice shouts at Lisa to run.

Carroll's classic was also referenced in the show's twenty-fourth annual Halloween special, "Treehouse of Horror," as film director Guillermo del Toro (*Hellboy*, *Pan's Labyrinth*) adds his unique twist to the opening "couch gag." After the family escapes from a series of monsters and villains (all drawn from a mash-up of iconic horror films), they plop on the couch. While this usually signals the end of the intro, in this case, Lisa falls through the couch and turns into Alice. Del Toro says of her tumble, "I integrate[d] Lisa falling through the couch like Alice in Wonderland but in the dress of the girl from *Pan's Labyrinth*, and instead of landing next to the giant toad in *Pan's Labyrinth*, she lands next to the Hypnotoad from *Futurama*. At the last minute I wanted to put a Mexican wrestler in there, but [casting director] Bonnie Pietila said to me, 'We've got to go! We cannot keep adding and adding stuff.' "

Other passing references occur in "Duffless" (Season 4), when Homer watches a driver's education film, starring Troy McClure, in traffic school, and McClure mentions another of his film credits, *Alice's Adventures through the Windshield*; "Lisa's Wedding" (Season 6), when Lisa follows a white rabbit to a fortune-telling booth; and "Moe Baby Blues" (Season 22), when Maggie wants Moe to read her *Alice in Wonderland*, but he turns her down, saying the book has "Chicks poppin' mushrooms."

CHAPTER 7
Alice in Books and Music

"When I used to read fairy-tales, I fancied that kind of thing never happened, and now here I am in the middle of one! There ought to be a book written about me, that there ought!"

—Lewis Carroll, *Alice's Adventures in Wonderland*

Lewis Carroll was among the first to adapt his own books, reworking *Alice's Adventures in Wonderland* into *The Nursery Alice* (1890) so that younger children could enjoy the story. Others soon flocked to join him, scribbling down hundreds of retellings, parodies, and sequels that continue to this day. These writers have sent Alice into other fantastical lands: some have had her meet up with old friends, such as the White Rabbit or the Hatter; others have introduced her to new friends. More than a few authors have used Alice to poke fun at the absurdities of politicians or the social mores of the day. Others have put Alice to didactic purposes, their adaptations instructing children how to parse sentences, identify musical instruments, and even to read.

Alice by the Book

A New Alice in the Old Wonderland

Written by Anna Matlack Richards. Illustrations by Anna M. Richards Jr. J.B. Lippincott Company. 1895.

Wife of William Trost Richards, a respected American landscape artist, Anna Matlack Richards (1835–1900) was also an artist in her own right, having published two books of sonnets for adults as well as a number of poems for children, printed in several well-regarded children's magazines of the day. In 1884, thirty years after the original *Alice's Adventures in Wonderland* appeared, J.B. Lippincott of Philadelphia published *A New Alice in the Old Wonderland*—Richards's children's novel that revisits Wonderland and pays tribute to Carroll's fantasy worlds.

The tale features another Alice, this time Alice Lee, an American child who dearly loves the Alice books and rereads them whenever she can. One moonlit night she sees in her bedroom "a door between the washstand and the table, where there had never been a door before." The door leads to more doors and soon Alice finds herself in Wonderland where she meets some of the characters from Carroll's two novels.

The book's sixty-seven illustrations were drawn by the author's daughter, Anna Richards Brewster—a successful impressionist, who painted landscapes, portraits, and still lifes. (In the book, Brewster is credited as Anna M. Richards Jr.) Brewster, heavily influenced by Tenniel's original drawings, did not attempt to alter his characters, which further strengthens the book's ties to the original source.

Left: Brewster's renderings of the Duchess and the Cheshire Cat rely heavily on Tenniel's interpretation.

Right: Frontispiece from *A New Alice in the Old Wonderland*.

PRICE SIXPENCE. WESTMINSTER POPULAR No. 18.

THE
WESTMINSTER ALICE.

BY

HECTOR H. MUNRO ("SAKI.")

ILLUSTRATED BY

F. CARRUTHERS GOULD.

The WESTMINSTER GAZETTE Office, Tudor-street, E.C.

Saki, a master of the short story, adopted his pen name in 1900, two years before *The Westminster Alice* was published.

Political Parodies

Starting in the early twentieth century, a number of writers used *Alice's Adventures in Wonderland* and *Through the Looking-Glass* as springboards to write about their own troubled times. These political parodies satirized and poked fun at political figures of the day.

One of the earliest to do so was *The Westminster Alice* (1902), a collection of vignettes first written for the *Westminster Gazette* by Hector Hugh Munro (1870–1916), better known by his pen name, Saki.

In the collection, Alice attempts to make sense of British politics, specifically the Boer War, which was then taking place in South Africa. In her role as an innocent child, Alice reveals British hypocrisy and complacency with the status quo. Francis Carruthers Gould (1844–1925), a political cartoonist, provided the book's forty-eight illustrations.

Another book critical of England's handling of the Boer War is *Clara in Blunderland* (1902), written by Caroline Lewis, a pseudonym for a trio of writers:

Lord Lansdowne, Secretary of State during the Boer War, portrayed as the White Knight, was satirized for his ineptitude and his reliance on outmoded weaponry. He justified sending troops into battle with ineffective guns by declaring, "If they happen to fall into the hands of the enemy they'd be very little use to him."

Harold Begbie, J. Stafford Ransome, and M. H. Temple. The following year, a sequel, *Lost in Blunderland* (1903), was published. In that parody, Arthur Balfour, the newly elected prime minister, is represented as Clara, now Queen of Blunderland, and struggling to put the kingdom to rights. J. Stafford Ransome, a journalist and one of the books' authors, did the illustrations for both books as well.

Another British parody is Charles Geake's *John Bull's Adventures in the Fiscal Wonderland* (1904). John Bull, a middle-aged British everyman, attempts to understand the economic climate of England; in the process, the book skewers leading British politicians. The illustrations are by Francis Carruthers Gould, who also did the drawings for *The Westminster Alice.*

The ability to poke fun isn't just a British characteristic. Americans, too, proved they could satirize with the best of them. John Kendrick Bangs

(1862–1922), an author and magazine editor, wrote *Alice in Blunderland: An Iridescent Dream* (1907). In this parody of corporate greed, Alice ends up in Blunderland, a new city founded by the Hatter, the March Hare, and the White Knight, and is confined against her will to the Municipal House of the Children, which the Duchess runs. Edward Hope, a writer for the *New York Herald Tribune*, penned *Alice in the Delighted States* (1928). In this parody of social foibles and hypocrisy, Alice finds herself transported to the Delighted States via the stem of a drinking glass. When Alice begins to grow, her clothes don't, and she is charged with indecent exposure. At her trial, presided by a judge who is literally wrapped in red tape, news of a sensational society murder interrupts the proceedings and Alice is let go. Rea Irvin, the *New Yorker*'s art editor at the time, did the illustrations.

The dedication to *Clara in Blunderland* reads, "With the most profound affection and respect to the memory of LEWIS CARROLL, to whom the author is as much indebted for the text as the illustrator to Sir John Tenniel for the ensuing parodies of his perfect pictures."

Didactic Alice

While Lewis Carroll was adamant that his Alice books be entertaining and not didactic, some of the many writers who have adapted his works have not shared his views. In *Gladys in Grammarland* (c. 1897), author Audrey Mayhew Allen sends the Verb Fairy to visit Gladys. Propelled through a cardboard door to Grammarland, Gladys becomes embroiled in a trial and is imprisoned for using incorrect grammar.

A book in the One Syllable Books series published by the A.L. Burt Company, *Alice's Adventures in Wonderland Retold in Words of One Syllable* (1905) retells Carroll's novel for beginning readers. In her adaptation, Mrs. J. C. Gorham uses mostly one-syllable words when recounting the adventures of Wonderland, although she does resort to hyphenating some longer words, most notably "A-lice."

American composer Ernest La Prada wrote *Alice in Orchestralia* (1925) to introduce children to the joys of the symphony orchestra. In the novel, Alice travels through a tuba to enter Orchestralia, where a bass viol is her guide to other animated musical instruments.

While the above books were all written before 1925, a more modern example exists as well. In 1995, Robert Gilmore's *Alice in Quantumland: An Allegory of Quantum Physics* was published. Instead of a rabbit hole, Gilmore's Alice falls through a television set straight into Quantumland, a place smaller than an atom. There she learns about electrons, energy fluctuations, and the uncertainty principle from a cast of unusual characters, such as the Uncertain Accountant and the Quark Brothers.

Unlike Carroll, many authors who adapted his work sought to educate their young readers.

Tweedledum and Tweedledee by Frances Broomfield.

New Adventures of Alice

Written and illustrated by John Rae. P. F. Volland Company. 1917.

In his novel, *New Adventures of Alice*, John Rae (1882–1963) starts with the final two sentences of *Through the Looking-Glass*. Betsy and her brother are listening to their mother reread their beloved book. When she comes to the end, Betsy sighs and says, "Oh dear, I wish there were more of it." Then she asks, "Isn't there another book about Alice, Mother?"

It is every book lover's secret dream to discover unknown books by a beloved author, and Betsy does just that later that night. Poking around the attic, she comes upon a set of Wish There Were More books, and in the pile of books that include *More Robinson Crusoe!* and More *Grimm's Fairy Tales!*, she finds the one she desires most of all—*More Adventures of Alice!* Betsy then proceeds to read the book, which begins with Alice lying outdoors on the grass reciting a Mother Goose rhyme, "Ding Dong Bell, Pussy's in the Well," to her kittens and leads to escapades with nursery rhyme characters, such as Old King Cole. Alice also meets a printer, a poet, and an artist in the course of her adventures.

Rae's black-and-white and full-color illustrations are reminiscent of Howard Pyle's drawings. Rae was a student of Pyle, who was deemed "the father of American magazine illustration" by the *New York Times*.

Original cover of the 1917 edition of the *New Adventures of "Alice."*

Dorothy Gale, Another Alice?

When L. Frank Baum composed his first Oz novel, *The Wonderful Wizard of Oz*, published in 1900, he was very much influenced by the story of a little girl who falls into a strange dreamscape, where she meets a number of bewildering characters and struggles to find her footing. Among the evidence that he based Dorothy Gale on Alice is a 1909 article he wrote, titled "Modern Fairy Tales," in which he praises Carroll, calling *Alice's Adventures in Wonderland* "one of the best and perhaps the most famous of all modern fairy tales." Comparing Carroll's heroine to Hans Christian Andersen's creations, Baum states, "The secret of Alice's success lay in the fact that she was a real child, and any normal child could sympathize with her all through her adventures."

Both Alice and Dorothy are notable for being ordinary children of their respective times. They are the "straight men" in the topsy-turvy worlds they find themselves in; although, tellingly, Baum has his creation come to love the inhabitants of Oz; whereas Alice never cares for Wonderland's citizens, and even actively dislikes quite a few.

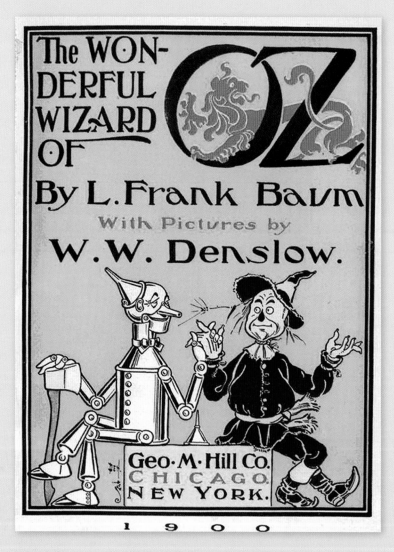

Baum never mentions Dorothy's age. In the original *The Wonderful Wizard of Oz*, her first illustrator, W.W. Denslow, pictures her as a young child of perhaps six or seven. John R. Neill, who illustrated the subsequent novels, shows her as a ten- or eleven-year-old. And in the 1939 film, sixteen-year-old Judy Garland plays her as a twelve-year-old.

"*You ought to be ashamed of yourself!*"

Two of Harry Trumbore's early studies for *Automated Alice* (top and bottom right) and *Star Wreck* (bottom left).

Alice Through the Needle's Eye: The Further Adventures of Lewis Carroll's Alice

Written by Gilbert Adair. E. P. Dutton. 1984.

Novelist and scriptwriter Gilbert Adair (1944–2011) was a Scotsman with a wide-ranging talent. Best known for novels such as *Love and Death on Long Island*, Adair is also noted for translating George Perec's novel *A Void* into English. Amazingly, the translation, like the original, does not contain the letter "e." This penchant for wordplay is evident in one of his earliest novels. In *Alice Through the Needle's Eye*, Adair pens a worthy tribute to Carroll. Adopting Carroll's surrealistic style, he uses the conceit of the alphabet to lead Alice through an amusing series of adventures. As she proceeds through the letters of the alphabet, Alice meets Ping and Pong, a pair of Siamese cats joined at the tail; Jack and Jill from nursery-rhyme fame; and her old friends the Red Queen and the White Queen. By the novel's end, Alice wakes and learns, as in Carroll's version, that it was all a dream.

Automated Alice

Written by Jeff Noon. Doubleday. 1996.

The conceit in this dystopian fantasy, a "trequel" to *Alice's Adventures in Wonderland* and *Through the Looking-Glass*, is that Lewis Carroll penned it. In truth, Jeff Noon, the British cyberfiction novelist and playwright, wrote the time-traveling tale, although he confesses that as he wrote: "I really felt Lewis Carroll was looking over my shoulder, correcting things, giving me ideas…Spooky!"

In the story, Alice is catapulted from Victorian Manchester into 1998, arriving in the future by means of the grandfather's clock that belongs to her Great Aunt Ermintrude. She finds herself in a strange universe populated by human/machine and human/animal hybrids, like Captain Ramshackle, half man and half badger. Ever resourceful, Alice attempts to make sense of her new surroundings while on the hunt for Great Aunt Ermintrude's parrot, Whippoorwill, whose escape from his cage is what has landed Alice in the future in the first place. Before long, Alice finds herself the prime suspect in a murder investigation. The unfortunate victims of the Jigsaw Murders are discovered with their parts artfully rearranged. With the help of an automated robot—the automated Alice of the title—Alice succeeds in solving the murders and returning to nineteenth-century Manchester. Or does she?

Noon, the winner of the 1994 Arthur C. Clarke Award (for the best science fiction book published in the UK) for his first novel *Vurt*, has fun toying with Carroll's fantasy world. Puns, puzzles, and wordplay abound as he details Alice's adventures in twelve chapters that loosely mimic the original. Harry Trumbore's black-and-white line drawings add amusing details that complement the story.

Still She Haunts Me

Katie Roiphe. Dial Press. 2001.

Nonfiction writer Katie Roiphe, daughter of the feminist writer Anne Roiphe, chose the relationship between Lewis Carroll and Alice Liddell as the subject of her first and only novel. The story starts with Carroll receiving a letter from Lorina Liddell, Alice's mother, in which she tells him: "It is no longer desirable for you to spend time with our family." This event did indeed happen to Carroll in 1863, when Alice was eleven, and Roiphe uses his rift with the Liddell family to explore the feelings Carroll had for young Alice and his inner turmoil. The central question of whether or not Carroll was a pedophile is left tantalizingly inconclusive.

Comics/Graphic Novels and Novelty Books

Alice in Sunderland: An Entertainment

Written and illustrated by Bryan Talbot.
Dark Horse. 2007.

An ambitious, sprawling epic of a book, Bryan Talbot's graphic novel is his love letter to Sunderland, a city in northeastern England, and the place that Talbot persuasively argues inspired Carroll to write his masterpieces. Among his proof is the Sunderland Museum where Carroll saw a stuffed walrus—the first time he encountered such a creature.

Drawing on centuries of British history, Talbot interlocked the chronicle of the Sunderland area with Lewis Carroll and his creation of the Alice books. Talbot starts by putting himself onstage as a performer at the Sunderland Empire Theatre; the only person in the audience is a bored member of the proletariat.

From the stage, Talbot then relates the history of Sunderland, going back six hundred million years or so and ending up in the present. But instead of a straightforward chronology, he jumps backward and forward in time, juggling multiple stories with the deftness of an acrobat. In addition to his pen-and-ink illustrations, Talbot employs photographs, paintings, and a range of mixed media—done in radically different styles—to create stunning visuals that explode off the page.

In an interview with *Comics Alliance*, Talbot said it wasn't until he moved to Sunderland in the late 1990s that he discovered that Lewis Carroll—as well as Alice Liddell—had "extensive links to the area and that many of the roots of Wonderland were firmly based in the North East." Four to five years in the making, Talbot's magnum opus won major acclaim when it was released in 2007. Danny Fingeroth, a comic book author and editor, went so far as to declare it "a candidate for the 'greatest graphic novel of all time.'"

Right: Talbot highlights E.T. Reed's cartoon "Tenniel's Alice Reigns Supreme" to show Tenniel's dominance over other illustrators.

Hatters often suffered brain damage caused by skin contact or inhalation of mercury, once used in the hat-making industry – a condition now known as *Mad Hatters' Syndrome.*

Tenniel remains *the* illustrator we associate with *Alice,* despite the hundreds of reinterpretations since the floodgates open on the lapse of copyright in 1907.

From the excellent Arthur Rackham to the delightfully idiosyncratic Mervyn Peake...

...from wacky Salvador Dali and whimsical Tove Jansson to visceral Ralph Steadman...

...thousands of changing images reinventing *Alice* each year in every passing style...

...yet Tenniel's vision reigns supreme, as prophesied in this 1907 *Punch* cartoon by ETReed.

Tenniel's *Alice* asks "Who are these funny little people?"

The Hatter replies "Your Majesty, they are your imitators."

176

Wonderland in DC Comics' *Batman*

The writers and cartoonists for DC Comics have frequently dipped into the Alice books for inspiration when creating their villains. The earliest—and most enduring—bad guy from the books is the Mad Hatter. Created by Bob Kane and Bill Finger, the Mad Hatter was born Jervis Tetch, a man obsessed with Carroll's *Alice in Wonderland*. Making his first appearance in *Batman* #49 of October 1948, Tetch tries to rob the members of Gotham's yacht club but is foiled by the caped crusader. A mad genius with the ability to control minds, Tetch now resides in an asylum for the criminally insane. The asylum must not be very secure because Tetch periodically escapes to wreak havoc.

In the ensuing decades, Tetch grows progressively darker. One of his more unsavory schemes is using subliminal messages to kidnap young girls—all blond—and sell them into slavery. His appearance has been altered as well, although he always wears his trademark hat. His height and hair color, though, have been changed repeatedly. Currently he has red hair, and much like Tenniel's original illustrations of the Hatter, an overly large head and buckteeth.

Dumfrey and Deever Tweed, aka Tweedledee and Tweedledum, are cousins—not brothers—who nevertheless bear a remarkable resemblance to each other. Leaders of a criminal organization, the pair first meet up with Batman and Robin during a crime spree in Gotham City. In issue #841 of *Batman: Detective Comics*, the cousins use the Mad Hatter's mind control devices to fool him into heading the Wonderland Gang, but really they are the ones pulling the strings.

Members of the Wonderland Gang include the Walrus and the Carpenter, the Lion and the Unicorn, and the Mad Hatter and the March Hare, all famous duos from Carroll's Alice books.

Then there is Alice herself, an enemy of Batwoman, as well as her evil twin sister, Elizabeth Kane. Alice, the leader of the Religion of Crime, speaks mainly in lines from *Alice in Wonderland*. In her last go-around with Batwoman, Alice falls from a plane into Gotham River. Presumably she dies, but as her body is never found, there is always the chance that the character will return.

TM and © DC Comics

Right: Born Jervis Tetch, DC's villain, The Mad Hatter, was a man obsessed with *Alice in Wonderland*.

Left: The cover of issue 841 in *Batman: Detective Comics* features cousins Dumfrey and Deever Tweed (aka Tweedledee and Tweedledum), the Mad Hatter, Batman, and more.

Lisa Comics: Lisa in Wordland! #1

Bongo Comics Group. 1995.

The only Simpsons comic book devoted solely to Bart's younger sister, *Lisa in Wordland!*, delightfully riffs on Carroll's original. Snowball, Lisa's cat, knocks Martin Gardner's *The Annotated Alice* off the bookcase and it conks Lisa on the head, right as she is in the middle of writing a letter, sending her off to dreamland—or rather, Wordland. Keen to post her letter, Lisa chases her White Rabbit, the bespectacled Ned Flanders, in his new role as letter carrier, throughout the word-obsessed landscape. She meets a new kind of dinosaur, a Thesaurus, who spouts polysyllabic words; goes to the home of the man who swallowed the dictionary, another logophile; and stops in a backward part of Wordland, where the local folk speak in palindromes. After refusing a drink of the letter "T" with the Mad Hatter (Sideshow Bob), Lisa has to cross the Land of Crosswords (an actual puzzle is included). Her last stop is the Gaming Grounds, where a giant Scrabble tournament is underway, with Mr. Burns as the letter tile "I"—a parody of the Queen of Hearts. As in the original, Lisa gets back to her own world by proclaiming the gamers "nothing but a bunch of stupid tiles," and upending the board, scattering the tiles. Great fun, this witty comic book invites frequent rereading.

Wordplay abounds in the first and only issue of *Lisa Comics*.

The Alice in Wonderland Cookbook: A Culinary Diversion

John Fisher. Clarkson N. Potter. 1976.

This cookbook offers up a compendium of recipes inspired by Carroll's two Alice books, such as Looking-Glass Cake, Not Too Dry Tea Biscuits, Mock Turtle Soup, and the Jam Tarts of the Queen of Hearts. Each recipe is accompanied with an excerpt from the book that inspired it. Illustrated with Tenniel's original drawings, the book also includes two of Carroll's shorter pieces: "Feeding the Mind," a write-up of a lecture he once gave, and "Hints for Etiquette: Or, Dining Out Made Easy." Published in 1855, the latter lists nine rules. Carroll offers such sage advice as:

"In proceeding to the dining room, the gentleman gives one arm to the lady he escorts—it is unusual to offer both."

"It is always allowable to ask for artichoke jelly with your boiled venison; however there are houses where this is not supplied."

"As a general rule, do not kick the shins of the opposite gentleman under the table, if personally unacquainted with him; your pleasantry is liable to be misunderstood—a circumstance at all times unpleasant."

According to a *Kirkus* review of the cookbook, "the dishes are generally rich, pleasant, and quite British."

Children's Books

Although Carroll's Alice books started out solely for children, by the 1920s and 1930s, they were appropriated more and more by the grownups. Literary artists, Freudian critics, and those in academia co-opted the books, directing their remarks to a sophisticated adult audience. Meanwhile, in today's popular culture, the books' characters are frequently portrayed in dark, sinister, and even sexualized terms.

But that doesn't mean that the books don't continue to hold an allure for children, although today's youth are probably more familiar with Disney's Alice than the original. Still, adaptations of the Alice books specifically written for younger readers continue to be released.

In the belief that one is never too young to be introduced to great literature, BabyLit has taken a number of classics and adapted them as board books for toddlers. One of the books in the series is *Alice in Wonderland: A BabyLit Color Primer*. Jennifer Adams's text paired with Alison Oliver's whimsical illustrations aim to teach toddlers their colors, starting with a white rabbit and ending with a yellow teapot.

While other pop-ups of *Alice in Wonderland* exist—such as Nick Denchfield's *Alice's Pop-up Wonderland* (2000) and J. Otto Seibold's *Alice's Adventures in Wonderland* (2003)—the definitive one has to be veteran paper engineer Robert Sabuda's 2003 version, which transforms the book into a bona fide toy. Each of its six action-packed spreads features a large three-dimensional detailed pop-up and a smaller mini-book that contains the text, as well as additional pop-ups. The abridged text remains true to Carroll's original and the full-color art respects the spirit of Tenniel's black-and-white illustrations.

Whoopi Goldberg starred as the Cheshire Cat in director Nick Willing's 1999 television movie of *Alice in Wonderland* (see page 92), so perhaps it shouldn't come as a surprise that seven years earlier the comedienne's first children's book featured an African-American Alice making her way across an urban landscape. This Alice travels by bus from New Jersey to downtown Manhattan to claim a cash prize that she is convinced will make all her dreams come true. Two friends accompany her—Robin, who is partial to hats, and Sal, an invisible white rabbit. While in the big city, Alice meets a handful of zany characters, rides the subway, and, of course, learns valuable lessons about prejudice, acceptance, and friendship. The 1992 picture book was illustrated by John Rocco.

Left: In the opening spread of Sabuda's pop-up—before Alice goes down the rabbit hole—the Cheshire Cat can be seen as a face in the trees.

Below: An *Alice in Wonderland* board book for toddlers.

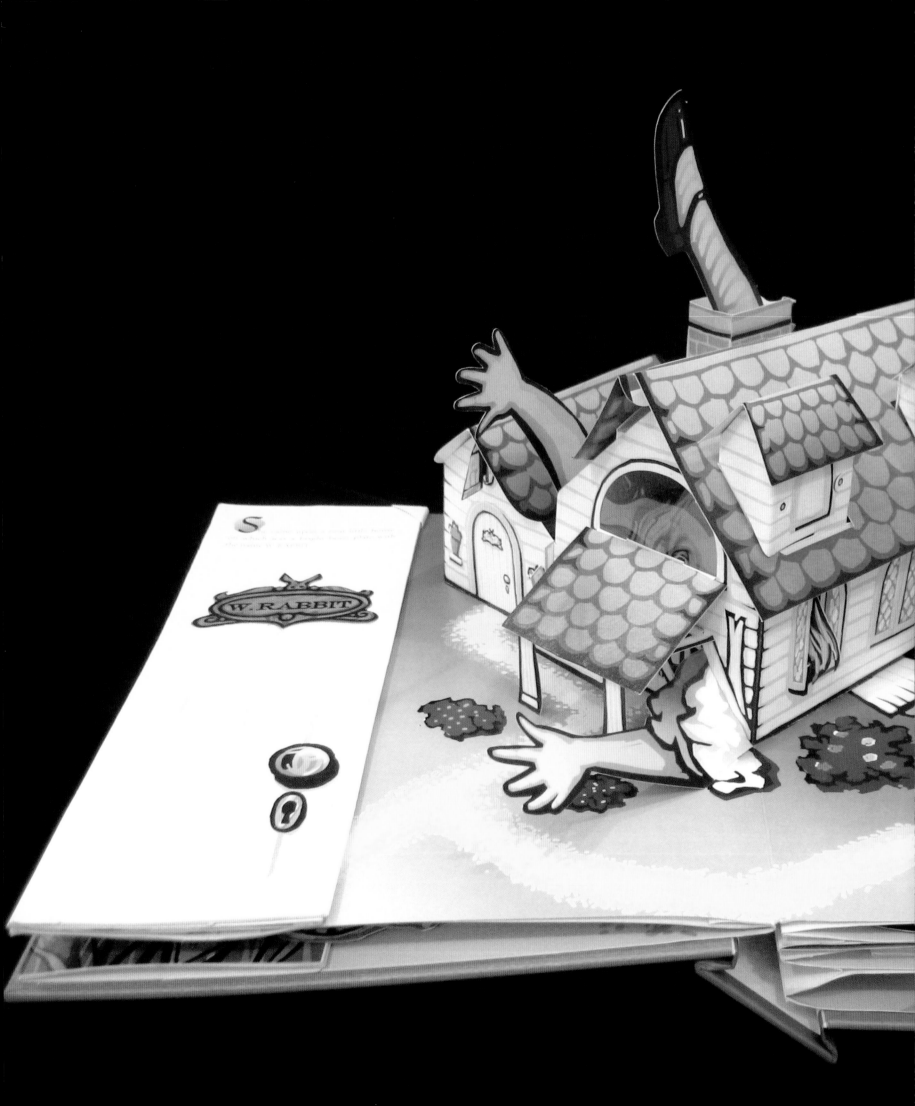

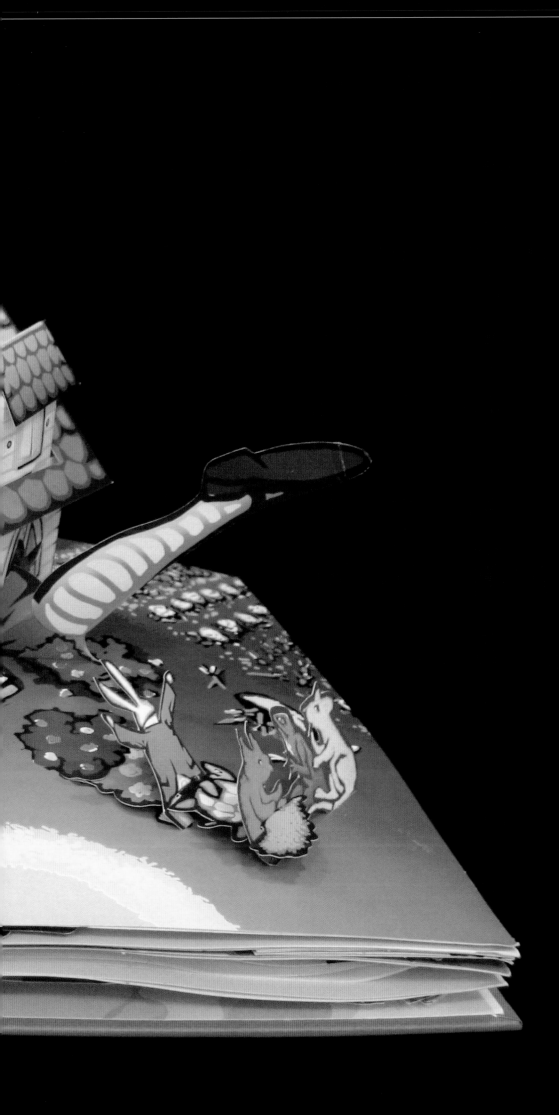

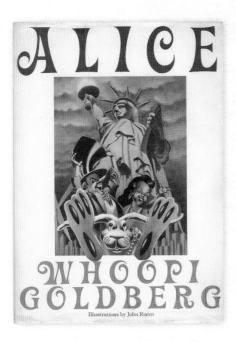

The cover of Whoopi Goldberg's *Alice*.

Alice outgrows the White Rabbit's
house in Sabuda's pop-up.

Above: In the final spread of Sabuda's pop-up, playing cards rise up to attack Alice.

Right: A colorful collection of *Alice* covers through the years.

In 2004, Chick-fil-A, a fast-food franchise, published a series of books called "Classic Stories & Essential Values," which the corporation distributed as part of its kids' meals. One of the books was a retelling of *Alice's Adventures in Wonderland* written by Mary Weber and illustrated by Isidre Mones. Unlike Carroll's original, which eschewed edifying morals, the Chick-fil-A version is described as "a story about the value of orderliness." While the twenty-four-page booklet does not tell Carroll's complete tale, it does a good job of introducing the main characters and scenes. In order to provide children with "essential values," the book's publisher saw fit to bowdlerize the classic. Many are minor changes: Alice eats cheese rather than pieces of mushroom, she's offered lemonade instead of wine at the Mad Tea Party, and the Dormouse is spared a dunking in the teapot. The most striking change, though, is that all references to beheadings have been deleted. In the place of the Queen of Hearts' famous "Off with his/her head" is the tepid "Put him/her behind bars." The booklet ends with three questions about order and rules for readers to ponder.

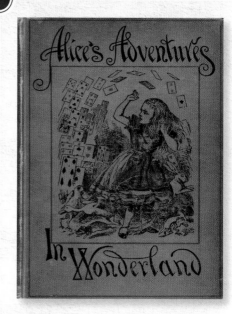

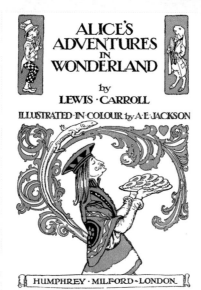

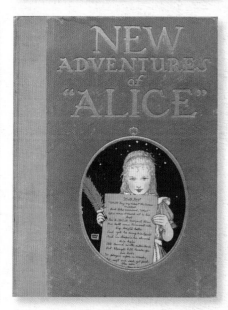

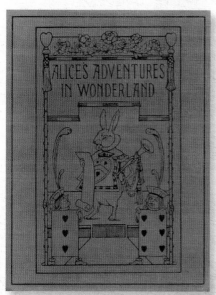

Whether or not "Lucy in the Sky with Diamonds" (right) references drugs, Lennon was mistaken about the boat scene coming from *Alice in Wonderland*. It comes from "Wool and Water" in *Through the Looking-Glass*.

Alice Set to Music

"You are sad," the Knight said in an anxious tone: "let me sing you a song to comfort you."

—Lewis Carroll, *Through the Looking-Glass*

While there are many poems in *Alice's Adventures in Wonderland* and *Through the Looking-Glass* for Alice to recite, there is very little singing. One of the few exceptions is the Mock Turtle, who sings two songs for Alice. One he warbles to her as he and the Gryphon dance to the Lobster Quadrille and the other is the mournful "Turtle Soup." If Carroll was remiss in composing more songs for Wonderland, a slew of songwriters have taken up the slack.

Songs

Songs that feature Alice include Neil Sedaka's 1963 hit, "Alice in Wonderland," in which the narrator tells his girl: "Tweedle dum, tweedle dee/You have made my life a fantasy/You don't know what you're doin' to me/My heart goes pitter patter/'Cause I'm mad as a hatter for/Alice my little girl." Alice isn't the only Wonderland character to get her own song, though. The Southern rock band Lynyrd Skynyrd dedicated the song Mad Hatter on their album *Vicious Cycle* to the memory of their bassist Leon Wilkeson, who died in 2001. The opening track of *Love and Theft*, Bob Dylan's 2001 album, is "Tweedle Dee and Tweedle Dum," a political song about America post 9/11

(some critics have interpreted the song as an allegory of the 2000 presidential election).

"Lucy in the Sky with Diamonds"

Sgt. Pepper's Lonely Hearts Club Band. Written by John Lennon/Paul McCartney. Capitol Records. 1967.

Picture yourself in a boat on a river
With tangerine trees and marmalade skies

Banned in the UK, "Lucy in the Sky with Diamonds" was considered by censors to be a song glorifying drug use. Many pointed to the fact that the initial letters in the song's title spelled out LSD. Lennon, who was the song's primary writer, contested that view, insisting that the title came from his four-year-old son Julian's drawing of a school friend named Lucy. As for the lyrics, Lennon claimed they were inspired by *Alice in Wonderland*. In a 1980 interview with *Playboy*, he told David Sheff, "The images were from *Alice in Wonderland*. It was Alice in the boat. She was buying an egg and it turns into Humpty-Dumpty. The woman serving in the shop turns into a sheep and the next minute they are rowing in a rowing boat somewhere and I was visualizing that."

"I Am the Walrus"

Magical Mystery Tour. Written by John Lennon/ Paul McCartney. Capitol Records. 1967.

Lennon composed this classic Beatles' song, written for the Magical Mystery tour, in August 1967, during the "Summer of Love." Released as a single on November 24, "I Am the Walrus" was on the B side, with "Hello, Goodbye" on the A side. The surreal lyrics caught the record-buying public by surprise and the song was a flop.

The inspiration for the song's title, as well as its recurring line, come from "The Walrus and the Carpenter," a poem that Tweedledee and Tweedledum recite for Alice in *Through the Looking-Glass*, one of Lennon's favorite books as a child. In an interview with *Playboy*, Lennon said:

"To me, it was a beautiful poem. It never occurred to me that Lewis Carroll was commenting on the capitalist and social system. I never went into that bit about what he really meant, like people are doing with the Beatles' work. Later, I went back and looked at it and realized that the walrus was the bad guy in the story and the carpenter was the good guy."

Interestingly, in *Through the Looking-Glass*, Alice, upon hearing the poem recited, initially likes the Walrus best, "because he was a *little* sorry for the poor oysters." Then Tweedledee reminds her that he ate more oysters than the Carpenter and Alice changes her mind, professing to prefer the Carpenter. Tweedledum tells her, "But he ate as many as he could get." Alice puzzles some more and finally pronounces them "both very unpleasant characters."

Another line in the song is thought by some to refer to *Through the Looking-Glass*. "I am the eggman," John sings in the third stanza. Is that a reference to Humpty Dumpty, another character from Carroll's second Alice book? Possibly, but just as possibly the line could refer to Eric Burdon, lead singer of the Animals, and someone whom Lennon nicknamed Eggman.

In *The Annotated Alice*, Martin Gardener questions whether Carroll intended the poem's political symbolism. He reminds the reader that when Carroll handed over the poem to Tenniel, he gave the illustrator the choice of illustrating the Walrus's sidekick as either a carpenter, a butterfly, or a baronet as he had no preference. Tenniel selected the carpenter.

"White Rabbit"

***Surrealistic Pillow*. Written by Grace Slick. RCA Victor. 1967.**

One of the Rock and Roll Hall of Fame and Museum's 500 Songs that Shaped Rock and Roll, "White Rabbit" was written in one hour in 1966 by Grace Slick, right before she joined Jefferson Airplane, a psychedelic rock band. The song, with vocals by Slick, was recorded in November 1966 and appeared on Jefferson Airplane's *Surrealistic Pillow* album. It was also released as a single. Its Spanish beat was influenced by Miles Davis and Gil Evans' *Sketches of Spain* album. But the lyrics came from Slick's "long-standing love affair with *Alice in Wonderland*."

Despite her affection for Carroll's works, Slick introduced errors into her lyrics. The final stanza reads:

Remember what the dormouse said
"Feed your head, feed your head

Yet in the book, it is the Queen of Hearts, not the Red Queen, who threatens to behead those who cross her and the White Knight doesn't do things backward; it's the White Queen. For that matter, the Dormouse never says, "Feed your head."

Although the song sneaked past the censors, from its first lines, "One pill makes you larger/And one pill makes you small," it references the drug experience. When Slick was questioned in a 2011 *Wall Street Journal* interview about whether the song is a metaphor for drugs, she replied:

"Not exactly. It's about following your curiosity. The White Rabbit is your curiosity. Alice follows him wherever he goes. He leads her to drugs, though, and that's why the song was written. Hey, all major

children's books do this. In *Peter Pan*, sparkle dust lets you fly. In the *Wizard of Oz*, they awaken in a poppy field to see the beautiful Emerald City. Our parents read us stories about chemicals that make it possible to have a good time."

Albums

The Mad Hatter

Chick Corea. Polydor. 1978.

All nine tracks that make up this jazz-fusion album reference Alice's journeys to Wonderland or Looking-Glass Land, as is obvious from the titles: "The Woods," "Tweedle Dee," "The Trial," "Humpty Dumpty," "Prelude to Falling Alice," "Falling Alice," "Tweedle Dum," "Dear Alice," and "The Mad Hatter Rhapsody."

Goodbye Alice in Wonderland

Jewel. Atlantic Records. 2006.

In 2006, singer/songwriter Jewel released an autobiographical album and single with the title *Goodbye Alice in Wonderland*. In an interview, she stated, "*Goodbye Alice in Wonderland* is no fairy tale, but still it is a strange trip indeed." The album, meant to represent a novel, with each of its thirteen tracks representing a chapter, was recorded live, although not in front of an audience. As she explained to *Rolling Stone* magazine, the album "tells the story of my life from Alaska to being homeless to that little bottle that said 'Drink me,' which was my career."

Alice

Tom Waits. Epitaph Records. 2002.

Originally composed as a musical for Hamburg's Thalia Theater Company in 1992, Waits' *Alice* was considered a lost masterpiece by critics because he never recorded the fifteen songs—not until 2002, that is, when the album was released. The play, the second in a trilogy by Robert Wilson, explores Carroll's complex relationship with Alice Liddell.

Waits, who wrote the songs with his wife, Kathleen Brennan, was lucky to have been able to release his album at all. The original tapes of the songs were stolen when a thief broke into Waits' car and held them for ransom. Waits ultimately paid $3,000 to get the tapes back, but they had already been bootlegged. It wasn't until years later that Waits looked at the tapes again and decided to record them on an album.

According to Waits, the songs—with titles such as "We're All Mad Here" and "Watch Her Disappear"— "aren't really a linear narrative"; instead, each piece can stand on its own. He said, *Alice* "is adult songs for children, or children's songs for adults. It's a maelstrom or fever-dream, a tone poem, with torch songs and waltzes…an odyssey in dream logic and nonsense."

Tom Petty's "Don't Come Around Here No More" Video (1985)

Directed by Jeff Stein, the video of "Don't Come around Here No More" won MTV's 1985 Best Special Effects at the Video Music Awards and was nominated for Video of the Year. Based on Carroll's *Alice's Adventures in Wonderland*, the video opens with Alice (Wish Foley) coming upon the sitar-playing Caterpillar, played by Dave Stewart (of the Eurythmics), the song's cowriter along with Tom Petty. Soon after, Alice finds herself as an unwanted guest at the Mad Tea Party. Petty, as a diabolical Hatter, ends up dunking a tiny Alice into his giant teacup (in actuality an aboveground pool artfully disguised). The video ends with Alice turned into a cake as Petty and the other band members consume her while she watches in horror. Because the video's ending caused a kerfuffle, an alternate version where Alice isn't eaten was filmed.

Tom Petty played the Hatter in the 1985 video.

Classical Alice

Through the Looking-Glass

Deems Taylor. 1918–1919.

While not as famous today as some other twentieth-century composers, such as Aaron Copland and George Gershwin, Deems Taylor (1885–1966) was well known—and well regarded—in his time. A music writer and critic as well as a composer, Taylor churned out operas, ballets, choral works, and chamber music. His inspiration lay in fantasy, and one of his orchestral suites is based on Carroll's second Alice book, *Through the Looking-Glass*.

Taylor's fondness for Carroll's books was grounded in his childhood. He reminisced, "I always did like fairy tales, and have liked both the Alice books since I first read them at age ten." He enjoyed them so much that he had a favorite game in which he and his friends competed to recite lines from the books. Playing the game, he "got to know the books even better, so it was quite natural that when I started to write my first serious symphonic piece of music, it should turn out to be the "Looking-Glass Suite."

For the piece, which he originally scored for a chamber orchestra and later for a full orchestra, Taylor chose five segments of Carroll's book: its dedication, a tender poem in praise of Alice Liddell; the talking flowers; the poem "Jabberwocky"; the Looking-Glass insects; and the White Knight.

"Through the Looking-Glass," performed by Carolyn Beebe and her New York Chamber Music Society, premiered at New York City's Aeolian Hall on February 18, 1919. The *Tribune*'s influential music critic was in the audience and praised the piece.

A critic for the *Guardian*, responding to a 1925 performance at the Leeds Music Festival in England, wrote that Taylor's "music runs along with a perfect security of invention and handling. It follows the ingenious invention as if the music had been born for no other purpose."

Taylor was Master of Ceremonies for Walt Disney's *Fantasia*. In addition to narrating the 1940 animated film, he helped to select the musical pieces that were performed.

An Alice Symphony (1969), Final Alice (1976), Child Alice (1980–1981)

David Del Tredici.

A review of David Del Tredici's works reveals at once the American composer's fascination with Carroll's two masterpieces. *An Alice Symphony* (1969), *Adventures Underground* (1971), *Vintage Alice* (1972), *Final Alice* (1976), and *Child Alice* (1977–1981) make up a significant portion of the artist's work. According to Del Tredici, "I felt I could set anything you told me was by Lewis Carroll—even his laundry list!"

Coming of age in the 1960s when the "military atonal" sound was prevalent in classical music, Del Tredici gradually found his work moving away from dissonance. By the time *Final Alice*, his best-known work—though not his last Alice piece!—was performed, Del Tredici had fully embraced lusher, more melodic compositions. *Final Alice*, like the earlier works, is concerned with Carroll's books and the events that occur in the stories. *Child Alice* takes a new direction, concentrating on Carroll and how he came to write the books. The concert's text comes from the prefatory poems that begin *Alice's Adventures in Wonderland* and *Through the Looking-Glass*. Each poem is viewed from two perspectives, a child's (Alice's) and an adult's (Carroll's).

After composing *In Memory of a Summer Day*, which was awarded a Pulitzer Prize in 1980, and the opera *Dum Dee Tweedle* (1991–1992), Del Tredici finally put Alice to rest and explored new subjects, most notably "The Spider and the Fly." In a 1998 interview with the *New York Times*, he confessed that at one point he was afraid to compose anything that wasn't Alice, stating, "I felt trapped by her, and thought I wouldn't be able to compose without an Alice text."

An illustration by Philip Mendoza from *Treasure* magazine (1966–67).

CHAPTER 8
Alice in Playland

"Why is a raven like a writing desk?"
—Lewis Carroll, *Alice's Adventures in Wonderland*

Playfulness permeates both Alice books, from the near constant wordplay to the games that are essential to their structure. Croquet and playing cards feature prominently in the first book as Alice navigates Wonderland and learns its strange rules—or its lack of them. In *Through the Looking-Glass*, chess is the dominant game, and Alice, who starts off as a lowly pawn, must play by its rules if she is to become a queen. Because fun and games are built into the books, it's only natural that almost immediately after they were published games based on them began to appear. The earliest ones were card games, the first coming out in 1882. Other games swiftly followed, including more card games, chess sets, board games, leading up to today's computer-based games and apps.

Lewis Carroll and Games

A lover of logic problems and wordplay, Carroll enjoyed composing mathematical puzzles and games to amuse himself and others. In 1870, seven of his puzzles appeared in *Aunt Judy's*, a children's magazine. The puzzles were originally written for young friends, such as this one for Mary Watson:

Dreaming of apples on a wall,
And dreaming often, dear,
I dreamed that, if I counted all,
—How many would appear?

Give up? Since he dreamed "often," or "of-ten," the answer is ten.

In the 1880s, Carroll wrote ten short stories in which mathematical problems figured prominently. The puzzles, or "knots," as Carroll referred to them, were first published in the magazine the *Monthly Packet*. Each story puzzle was published without its solution, and Carroll invited readers to send in theirs. He then provided the correct answer in a later edition and commented—not always flatteringly—on his readers' responses. In 1885, Carroll published the collected stories in a book titled *A Tangled Tale* with illustrations by Arthur Frost.

In addition to his enjoyment of mathematical puzzles, Carroll was a fan of acrostics and created acrostic poems in which the first letter of each line spells out a word, usually a name. *Through the Looking-Glass* includes an elaborate example of such an acrostic: In "A Boat Beneath a Sunny Sky," Carroll's recollection of the July boat ride that set both Alice books in motion and the poem that ends the book, the initial letters of the lines spell out ALICE PLEASANCE LIDDELL.

If more proof is needed of Carroll's inventive mind, then consider that he also came up with Doublets, a word puzzle that appeared in an 1879 issue of *Vanity Fair*. The game captured the imagination of Victorians and became quite the fad in London for a time. The game is still played, although it is better known today as Ladders. Its rules are simple: Take a word and turn it into another word of the same length by changing just one letter at a time. Each letter change must also form a new word. The first Doublet Carroll created for *Vanity Fair* changed HEAD into TAIL thus:

HEAD—HEAL—TEAL—TELL—TALL—TAIL.

Right: A selection of Alice playing cards from Thomas De La Rue & Co in 1899 (see page 159).

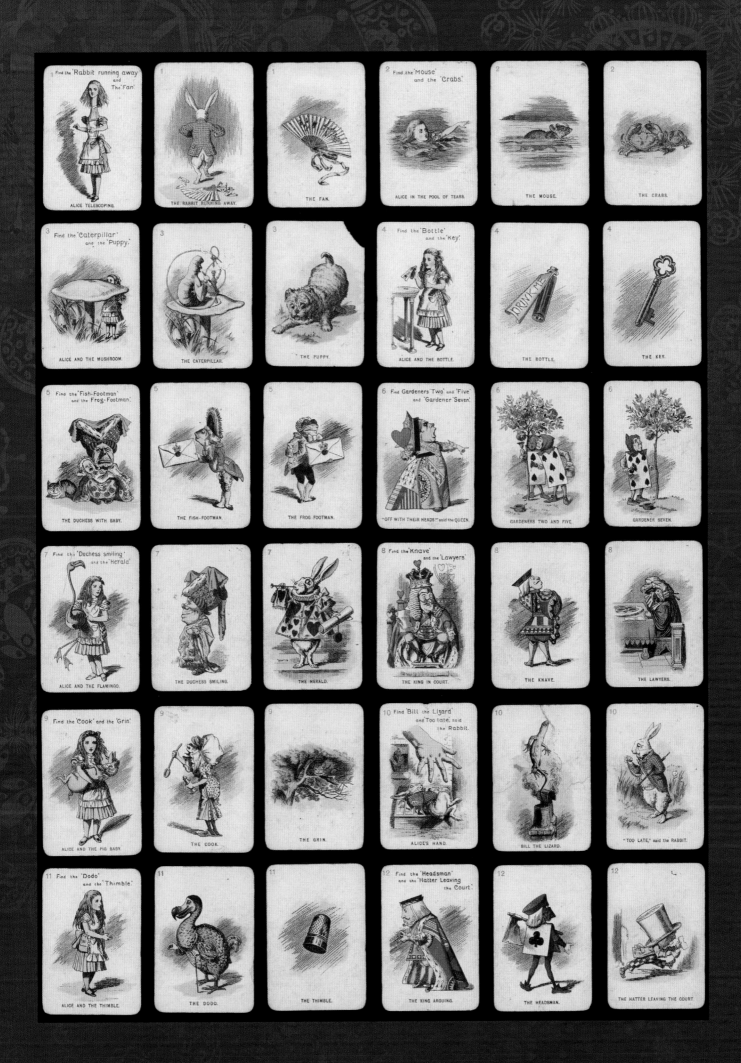

The Answer to the Hatter's Riddle

So why *is* a raven like a writing desk? At the Mad Tea Party the Hatter claims he hasn't "the faintest idea." Readers, however, weren't satisfied with that response and pestered Carroll to provide a solution. In a preface he wrote for the 1896 edition of *Alice's Adventures in Wonderland*, he stated that the riddle "as originally invented" had "no answer at all." Nevertheless, he came up with "a fairly appropriate" one: "Because it can produce few notes, tho they are *very* flat; and it is never put with the wrong end in front!" But while the first half of the answer made sense, the second part continued to baffle people.

It wasn't until 1976 that the mystery was solved. Denis Crutch wrote in *Jabberwocky*, a publication put out by the Lewis Carroll Society of North America, that Carroll originally had spelled "raven" backward, so the riddle actually reads, "Because it can produce few notes, tho they are *very* flat; and it is nevar put with the wrong end in front!" Crutch posited that an editor figured the "nevar" misspelling to be a typo and emended it (much like today's autocorrect). Carroll's response, however, didn't stop people with coming up with their own answers. Among the more famous ones are Aldous Huxley's "Because there's a 'b' in both, and because there is an 'n' in neither," and chess player and puzzle author Sam Loyd's suggested, "Poe wrote on both."

Card Games

At the end of *Alice's Adventures in Wonderland*, as Alice is at the trial for the Knave of Hearts and soon to awake from her dream, she responds to the Queen's shout of "Off with her head!" with a disdainful "Who cares for you? You're nothing but a pack of cards!" The cards then attack Alice as if in a spirited game of 52 Pickup. It is fitting then that the first *Alice in Wonderland* game should be a card game. The Game of Alice in Wonderland came out in 1882 and featured fifty-two cards that displayed Tenniel's Wonderland characters. The cards were divided into two sets of sixteen numbered picture cards and one set of twenty numbers-only cards. Produced by Selchow & Righter, a British firm, the game was for two to six players. After the cards are dealt, players take each other's cards according to ranking. The player with the most cards wins.

Before the century ended, Parker Brothers came out with its Wonderland card game in 1895, followed by the Alice in Wonderland card game by the McLoughlin Bros. in 1898. In 1899, Thomas De La Rue & Co.'s The New & Diverting Game of Alice in Wonderland hit the market with illustrations by E. Gertrude Thompson, a friend of Carroll's and the cover illustrator for *The Nursery Alice*.

In 1930, the Carreras Tobacco Company gave away an Alice in Wonderland card with each pack of cigarettes, hoping to entice smokers to buy their brand. The idea was to collect the whole set. There was one catch, though: you had to buy the rules in order to find out how to play the game.

One year after Walt Disney's 1951 animated *Alice in Wonderland* movie was released, Pepys printed its Alice in Wonderland card game featuring the Disney characters. For two to six players, the aim was to collect sets of cards that have the same letters in the circles.

Left: The box cover to the Thomas De La Rue & Co.'s cards featuring illustrations by E. Gertrude Thompson.

Below: An Alice playing card distributed by Carreras Tobacco Company in 1930.

Carroll's Croquet

The game of croquet took Victorian England by storm in the 1860s. A new game brought over from France, it captivated Lewis Carroll, who enjoyed playing it with members of his family, and, from time to time, with the young Liddell sisters. Because the rules for the game were in flux, Carroll devised his own version and published it in 1863 as *Croquet Castles: For Five Players*. He later revised the game to include just four players. No matter four players or five, his version was a complicated one and never really caught on.

Chess Sets

While *Alice's Adventures in Wonderland* features a deck of cards, its sequel uses the game of chess as its underlying motif. Structured like a chess game, the beginning of *Through the Looking-Glass* establishes Alice as a pawn. In her quest to become Queen, she must make her way across a large chessboard. The squares of the boards consist of fields with the rows separated from each other by brooks, and the columns divided by hedges.

To underscore how important chess is to the story, Carroll included a diagram of a chess game that illustrates the moves Alice makes. When more than a few readers professed puzzlement as to its accuracy, Carroll wrote a preface to the 1897 edition explaining himself. In it he admits that the "*alternation* of Red and White is perhaps not so strictly observed as it might be" but he insists that those who "take the trouble to set the pieces and play the moves as directed" will find them "to be strictly in accordance with the laws of the game."

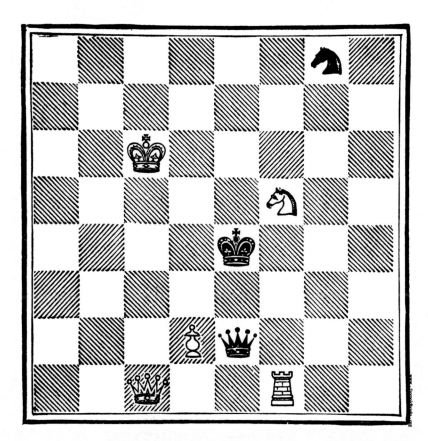

Above: This chess diagram appears in the preface to the 1897 edition of *Through the Looking-Glass*.
Above left: An example of Lewis Carroll's croquet as depicted in Jonathan Barry's *The Queen of Hearts*.

Tenniel's Chessboard

In 2011, Jake Fior, a British rare-book seller, made a fortuitous discovery. In each corner of the antique chessboard he had recently purchased were the initials JT. The chessboard's border is hand-painted with sixteen ink and watercolor illustrations featuring characters from *Through the Looking-Glass*. Fior did some research and learned that John Tenniel had signed many of his drawings in the same manner. A conservator from London Metropolitan University confirmed Fior's suspicions; the one-of-a-kind chessboard was indeed by Alice's first illustrator. What inspired Tenniel to create the chessboard? No one knows that answer, but Fior speculates that it might have been a onetime commission or perhaps Tenniel was entertaining thoughts of producing Alice merchandise.

Right: Illustrated chessboard created by John Tenniel.
Below: A detail of the Lion and the Unicorn.

Alice Chess Set (2008)

Place one of Yasmin Sethi's opaque chess pieces on her specially designed board and something magical happens: the piece becomes transparent and its identity is revealed. Removed from the board, the piece reverts to being opaque and indistinguishable from the rest of the set. Inspired by *Alice's Adventures Through the Looking-Glass*, Sethi, a designer, created a prototype of the chess set to illustrate how a chess piece is valueless unless it is in play.

The silhouettes of standard Staunton chess figures are enclosed inside the glass chess pieces. When one of the pieces is set down on a square, the glass board, studded with embedded LEDs, lights up and the silhouette is instantly visible.

The four knights are the only chess pieces to appear upside down. That's because in *Through the Looking-Glass* the White Knight professes to think better when he is upside down.

Role-Playing Games

Dungeonland and The Land Beyond the Magic Mirror

TSR. Created by Gary Gygax. 1983.

One of the first role-playing games to take hold was Dungeons & Dragons. Created in 1974 by Gary Gygax, who was considered by many to be the father of fantasy role-playing games, it set off an avalanche of gamers clamoring to go on campaigns and adventures. Each player has his or her own persona, a player character (PC), while the game master has the challenging job of running the adventure and acting as the referee when needed.

In 1983, Gygax came out with Dungeonland—"an adventure in a wondrous place"—that was inspired by *Alice's Adventures in Wonderland*. With a roll of the die, the adventurers venture into the strange land—down the Endless Shaft, through the Long Hall, and into the Tiny Garden. From there, they must pass through the Woods of Trees and Giant Fungi and the Wilds of Dungeonland before reaching the Palace. In each place, the PCs face situations based on episodes from Wonderland—for instance, they swim across the Pool of Tears, play a deadly game of croquet, and face a trial at the royal palace—and meet its inhabitants, who have been converted into Dungeons & Dragons–equivalent characters; hence, the Cheshire Cat is a saber-toothed tiger, the Caterpillar a behir, and the March Hare a lycanthrope.

In the game's afterword, Gygax writes that in order to get the most out of his game, ". . . the Gentle Reader is urged to read Lewis Carroll's story, *Alice in Wonderland*. Read this book carefully. You might even find you enjoy sections sufficiently to reread them."

That same year also saw the publication of The Land Beyond the Magic Mirror, Gygax's version of *Through the Looking-Glass*, and PCs got to partake in a chess game while rubbing elbows with the Jabberwock, the Bandersnatch, and the Walrus and the Carpenter.

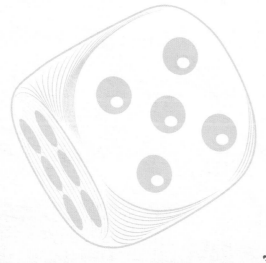

Electronic/Computer Games

Alice in Wonderland

Digital Eclipse Software. 2000.

Disney's 1951 animated *Alice in Wonderland* was transformed into a video game in 2000. Designed for Nintendo's Game Boy Color, the platform video game is faithful to the Disney version and even includes cut scenes from the movie. After a brief setup, a player (represented by Alice) falls down a rabbit's hole and enters Wonderland. There, over the course of more than twenty levels, Alice faces a number of side-scrolling challenges as she hops, jumps, and leaps over obstacles and helps the denizens of Wonderland find lost objects. To accomplish some goals, she must alter her size with the magic mushrooms she picks up along the way.

Alice in Wonderland

Disney Interactive Studios. 2010.

Unlike other *Alice in Wonderland* games, players of this Tim Burton version aren't in control of Alice; instead, they assume the roles of various Wonderland (or Underlandian) characters in her quest to defeat the Jabberwock. Made for three different platforms—PC and Nintendo Wii and DS—the Wii and PC versions feature a visual style reminiscent of the movie, with its color-saturated, naturalistic animation. The DS, on the other hand, has a cartoony look with its stark black-and-white edges and its minimalist use of color. Also, in the DS version, there are only four characters you can maneuver (the Mad Hatter, the White Rabbit, the Caterpillar, and the Cheshire Cat), while in the other two platforms there are five (the Mad Hatter, the White Rabbit, the March Hare, the Dormouse, and the Cheshire Cat).

The play for all three games, though, is basically the same. Players switch among the Wonderland characters as they guide, protect, and help Alice progress through the levels to face her final enemy—the Jabberwock. Each character has its own unique ability, which adds to the fun. The White Rabbit, for instance, can control time, and the Cheshire Cat can make certain objects disappear.

Surprisingly, perhaps, the handheld DS version of the game received higher marks than the more visually stunning Wii and PC versions. Reviewers praised its engaging puzzle-solving aspects and its stylized design. The Wii and PC versions were not as highly rated with critics, who cited the repetitive combat fighting and occasional glitches in the visuals, especially during the cut scenes. Some of the film's cast appear as voice actors, including Mia Wasikowska (Alice), Crispin Glover (the Knave of Hearts), and Stephen Fry (the Cheshire Cat).

American McGee's Alice

Rogue/Electronic Arts. 2000. *Alice: Madness Returns*. **Spicy Horse/Electronic Arts. 2011.**

"Wonderland's become quite strange," Alice remarks to the Cheshire Cat in a cut scene from *American McGee's Alice*, a computer video game released in 2000. "Strange" is an understatement. It is 1874 in this sequel to the Alice books, and Wonderland has become a macabre and creepy place whose inhabitants have become warped and twisted. The backstory to the game is suitably Gothic as well. Young Alice's parents have died in a fire, caused by her cat, Dinah, knocking over an oil lamp. Alice escaped by jumping out through a window onto a snowbank; but now she's a teenager lying catatonic in a psychiatric asylum, consumed with guilt.

In the game's opening scenes, a nurse places Alice's old stuffed toy, a white rabbit, next to her rigid body. As Alice moves to cuddle it, the toy comes to life, beseeching her to "Save us, Alice!" The pair tumble down a chute and land on a pile of leaves. From then on, Alice must use her wits as she navigates Wonderland and tries to kill the evil Queen of Hearts who dominates the underground realm. By defeating the Queen and restoring peace to Wonderland, Alice is also repairing her sanity.

The gamer controls Alice's avatar, the game's only playable character. With the Cheshire Cat, a skinny and malevolent-looking creature, as her guide, Alice collects various weapons (blunderbuss, croquet mallet, and Vorpal Blade, among others), which she then uses to defend herself from the enemies that she meets as she searches for the Queen of Hearts. If the gamer is not successful, Alice dies—going up in flames, drowning, or in some other horrible manner. Then the gamer must restart the level and try again.

Game maven American McGee (*Dune* and *Quake*) designed *Alice* and was rewarded with having his name included in the title. McGee admits that the bizarre nature of his game was in part inspired by his unorthodox childhood. "It was like 1,000 episodes of Sally Jessy Raphael," he says in an interview with Noah Shachtman of *Wired*. Chris Vrenna, a member of the band Nine Inch Nails, composed the otherworldly music that haunts the game.

American McGee's Alice received high praise after its release and has gone on to become one of the more popular action-adventure games with a devoted fan base. Its imaginative visuals received special mention, with a reviewer in the *New York Times* stating that it is "as much fun to look at as it is to play." However, some gamers reported being disappointed with the lack of challenges. A reviewer for *GamePro* put it bluntly: "It's fun for a while, but the overly simplified game mechanics and repetitive shoot-and-run gameplay wouldn't amount to much without the extraordinary visuals and awesome concept."

Eleven years after *American McGee's Alice*, its sequel was released. Designed for the computer as well as for PlayStation and Xbox, *Alice: Madness Returns* picks up one year after the first game ends. Released from the asylum, Alice is now under the care of a psychiatrist who is helping her forget painful memories and hallucinations. According to American McGee, the story resembles a murder mystery in that Alice attempts to discover what happened on the fateful night her family was killed in the fire. Responding to concerns that fans of *American McGee's Alice* raised, McGee upgraded the new game's combat system and its difficulty levels. Although some reviewers felt that the game was more enjoyable to look at than to play, it received mostly positive reviews.

At the beginning of *American McGee's Alice*, young Alice, now a teenager, is confined to a psychiatric asylum.

An illustration by *Alice in Wonderland* fan artist Zsófia Szabó.

Apps

Alice for the iPad

Atomic Antelope. 2010.

Introduced in April 2010, *Alice for the iPad* is one of the most popular children's storybook apps ever created. More than 500,000 readers have installed the app on their tablets, making it one of the top-grossing children's book apps. Chris Stevens, a former journalist and graphic designer, who co-created the app along with programmer Ben Roberts, credits its success to the "great content" provided by Carroll and Tenniel, and to its unique interactive approach. With the app, users can engage with Tenniel's illustrations as never before. By manipulating the tablet, they can make Alice grow and shrink with the swipe of a finger, throw tarts at the Queen of Hearts, and send playing cards flying.

The updated app contains both a 52-page abridged version and a 249-page full-length edition of *Alice's Adventures in Wonderland*. Stevens handled the graphics and design while Roberts did all the programming. The result is "a kind of digital pop-up book" that, according to *Kirkus*, "makes it a powerful demonstration of the iPad's storytelling ability."

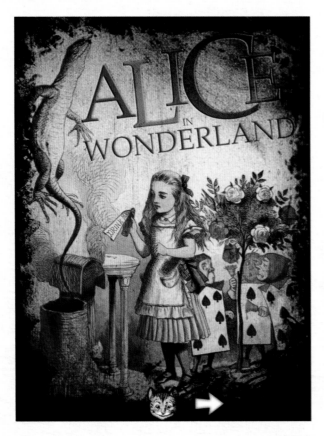 

The "cover" and one of the "pages" from *Alice for the iPad*.

Alice in New York

Atomic Antelope. 2011.

A mash-up of *Through the Looking-Glass* and iconic 1930s New York City, *Alice in New York* is another interactive app from Chris Stevens, who wanted to create something special in honor of the 140th anniversary of Carroll's sequel. Stevens chose New York over other cities because he was struck by how closely "Manhattan could be retrofitted onto the original Lewis Carroll book with supernatural accuracy." The chessboard fields in *Through the Looking-Glass* are re-created in the orderly grid of New York City streets, and characters from the book reappear in new guises.

The Red Queen is now a red-cloaked Statue of Liberty. Tweedledee and Tweedledum are taxi drivers, and Humpty Dumpty teeters on a construction girder high above the city.

Stevens adapted Carroll's text and hired illustrator Petra Kneile to create drawings in Tenniel's style. The interactive features include a spin on the Coney Island Ferris wheel, a subway ride on a graffiti-scrawled train, and a stunning fireworks display. The most impressive feature, perhaps, comes at the end with an illustration of the pint-size Red Queen/Statue of Liberty in Alice's hands. When the user shakes the tablet she changes into a black kitten, just as in Carroll's book.

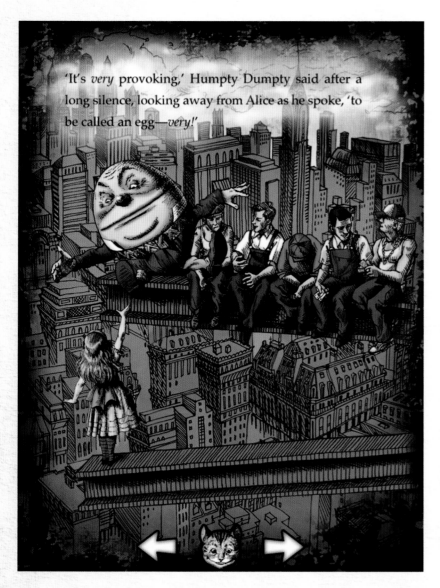

By tilting the tablet, users can cause Humpty Dumpty to sway or the Statue of Liberty to tilt.

Alice in Ads

According to a 1922 advertisement, during Alice's visit to Wonderland, she "found nothing so delicious as Post Toasties." Post promoted its cereal as a food source that would help children grow. "Not teeny, weeny, or not great big. But just right."

Advertisements using Alice's iconic image had their heyday in the late 1940s and continued throughout the early 1950s. She was used to sell everything from cars, refrigerators, and television sets to life insurance, grape juice, and telephones.

Perhaps the most well-known—and surprising—product Alice hawked was Guinness beer. In addition to standard advertisements, Guinness produced five limited-edition Alice-themed booklets between the years 1933 and 1959. The promotional booklets were sent to doctors around Christmastime as an appreciation and also to encourage them to spread the word about the benefits of drinking Guinness. (To add credibility to its "Guinness is Good for You" campaign, the company had sought testimonials from doctors.) The illustrated booklets featured parodies of characters from the Alice books and worked in numerous references to Guinness. Carroll's poem "Father Williams" is spoofed in the first booklet, *The Guinness Alice*.

"You are old Father William," the Young Man said,
"And yet you're remarkably fit,
You sleep from the moment you get into bed,
Which is rare at your age, you'll admit."
"In my youth," said the Sage, "I heard many reports
That Guinness brought rest to the brain,
Since when, if depressed or a bit out of sorts,
I've drunk it again and again."

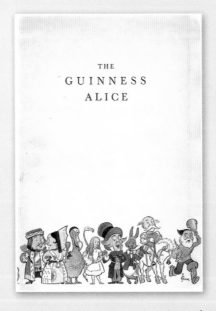  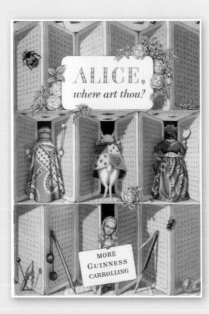

Guinness' promotional booklets about Alice are highly collectible.

The Guinness Birthday Book

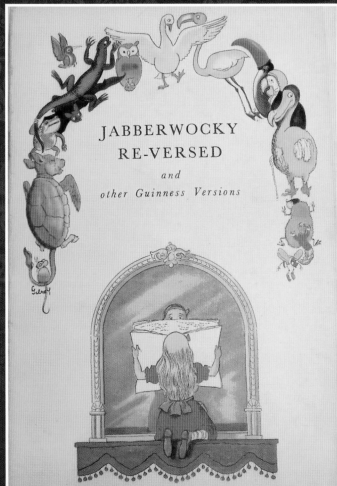

JABBERWOCKY
RE-VERSED
and
other Guinness Versions

Catch as catch can't

"He runs with all his might," panted the Lion, "but I run with might and mane, you know."

"My Goodness," Alice exclaimed, "you *are* fast."

"Your Goodness — *puff* — my dear young lady — *puff* — has nothing to do with it," said the Lion. "It's the Keeper's Goodness I'm after — the Goodness in his Guinness. I haven't the strength to catch him till I've had a Guinness."

"But you can't have the Guinness till you catch him," Alice objected.

"I know," said the Lion. "That's what makes me such a *wild* animal."

G.E. 1440.B.

"OFF WITH THEIR HEADS!" said the QUEEN.

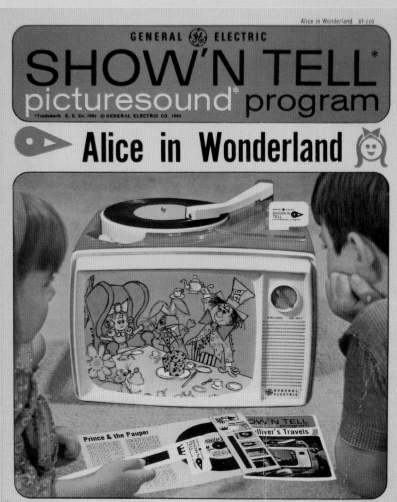

An articulated paper doll, jigsaw puzzle, and filmstrip viewer from the 1960s are just a few of the countless toys based on *Alice in Wonderland*.

Child's Play

From board games and puzzles to dolls, tea sets, and costumes, a host of Alice merchandise exists that caters specifically to children.

Some of the earliest *Alice in Wonderland* dolls were crafted by Martha Jenks Chase, an accomplished seamstress from Rhode Island, who channeled her talent with the needle into a successful doll-making business. Chase believed that the mechanical dolls that were increasingly filling toy store shelves around the turn of the twentieth century inhibited imaginative play, so in 1899, she set about making molded cloth dolls that children could cuddle. Made from a cotton knit called stockinet, the lightweight dolls had their features painted on with washable paints and were sold in departments stores, like Macy's, as well as in toy stores. In 1905, Chase came out with a line of dolls featuring characters from *Alice's Adventures in Wonderland* and *Through the Looking-Glass*, including Alice, the Hatter, the Duchess, and Tweedledee and Tweedledum.

Since then, other doll makers and toy companies have made Alice dolls, including Madame Alexander (who at the start of her career in the 1920s fashioned handmade Alice dolls out of cloth), Ginny, and Pedigree. Not to be left out, Mattel has produced a number of Alice dolls through the years. In 2007, the company issued a Barbie Alice, a brunette who sports a ruffled blue dress and comes with a model of the Cheshire Cat.

A simple puzzle game featuring some of Carroll's beloved characters.

Left: A collection of Martha Chase's dolls, starting from the far left: Alice, the Frog Footman, Tweedledee and Tweedledum, the Duchess, and the Hatter.

Below: Made from cloth or porcelain, Alice dolls continue to appeal to children and collectors alike.

Alice in Wonderland Statue in Central Park

Its official title is the *Margarita Delacorte Memorial* but park-goers in New York City know it as the *Alice in Wonderland* statue. George Delacorte, a successful publisher and philanthropist, was grief-stricken when his wife, Margarita, died. She had always loved Carroll's nonsense books and read them often to the couple's children, her favorite being the poem "Jabberwocky." As a tribute to his wife, Delacorte commissioned a statue of *Alice in Wonderland.* The Spanish sculptor José de Creeft created the bronze piece, designing it so that children could scramble atop it. After Robert Moses dedicated the statue in May 1959, opening it to the public, children took to it immediately. Over the years, the sculpture has been so beloved by children that their hands have polished sections of the bronze surface smooth.

Located in Central Park, not far from East 74th Street, the statue stands eleven feet high and features Alice, her cat, Dinah, in her lap, perched atop a giant mushroom and surrounded by four Wonderland characters: the White Rabbit, the Cheshire Cat, the Hatter, and the Dormouse. Except for Alice, all were patterned after Tenniel's illustrations. Seven bronze tablets—six bearing an inscription from Carroll's books and one a dedication plaque to Margarita Delacorte—can be found around the statue's base.

De Creeft used his daughter, Donna, as the model for Alice.

CHAPTER 9
Alice in the Modern World

*"But it's no use going back to yesterday, because
I was a different person then."*

—Lewis Carroll, *Alice's Adventures in Wonderland*

Lewis Carroll wrote about Alice and her adventures in a world very different from today. Women wore stiff crinoline dresses that swept the floor, while men donned top hats and walking sticks. They traveled by horse-drawn carriages and railway, and corresponded through handwritten letters. Yet, despite all the differences, his books have endured. In our modern world, they continue to inspire a flurry of products—Wonderland teacups and trinkets and T-shirts and nail polish—for a public eager to consume them. There are Alice-themed restaurants, Alice tattoos, and even a medical syndrome based on his works, called Alice in Wonderland Syndrome, which is a neurological condition that affects perception and is often associated with migraines. And as the world changes, so does Alice. Today she can be found as a steampunk heroine, between the pages of a manga comic book, and in software designed to help children learn to program 3-D animation.

Disney Rides and Attractions

In spite of Walt Disney's dissatisfaction with his 1951 animated film (see page 106), he nevertheless made sure that his theme parks included *Alice in Wonderland* rides. After his death, more parks opened and they too welcomed Alice-themed attractions to draw in guests.

The Mad Tea Party Ride

When Disneyland opened in Anaheim, California, on July 17, 1955, one of the attractions was inspired by the animated movie. The Mad Tea Party ride consists of eighteen teacups set upon three turntables that fit within a larger turntable. The smaller turntables rotate clockwise, while the larger turntable spins counterclockwise. In addition, each teacup has its own wheel, which allows riders to make their cup spin faster. All this spinning can make the one-and-a-half-minute ride seem like an eternity if you suffer from motion sickness.

Today the ride appears at all five Disney theme parks (California, Florida, Paris, Tokyo, and Hong Kong) with minor variations.

Teacups twirl underneath a petal-shaped glass roof at the Disney park in Paris.

Alice in Wonderland Ride

Unique to Disneyland, the Alice in Wonderland attraction takes visitors on a railway tour through scenes of Wonderland. Passengers hop aboard a caterpillar-style ride and chug down the rabbit hole and through a door to see familiar animated characters such as the Cheshire Cat, the Caterpillar, and the Queen of Hearts. Songs from the film play throughout the journey, and Kathryn Beaumont, who was the voice of Alice, provides the commentary. The ride was introduced in 1958, but in 1983, it underwent a renovation and was spiffed up with some rooms eliminated and others added.

Alice's Curious Labyrinth

Toward the end of Disney's *Alice in Wonderland*, the Queen of Hearts chases Alice through a maze. (No such maze appears in either of Carroll's Alice books.) Alice's Curious Labyrinth, an amusement park attraction at Disneyland Paris that opened in 1992, uses this scene as its inspiration. The labyrinth, which is made up of winding hedges, has two sections. The first—and easier—maze starts at the entrance and leads to Tulgey Wood. There, visitors are greeted by animatronic Disney creatures from the film, including the Accordion Owl, Horn Ducks, and a Hammer Bird. The Cheshire Cat, true to its mysterious nature, pops up throughout the park, speaking droll phrases in French. After visitors have traipsed through the Caterpillar's Mushroom Lair and Caucus-Race section, they come to a divide. One leads to the Cheshire Cat Walk, the other to the Queen of Hearts Maze. The latter with its high hedge-walls and eight dead ends is decidedly more challenging, as a sign held by a model of the Cheshire Cat proclaims: "May Be Difficult. You Could Lose Your Head!" Eventually, the maze leads to the Queen's castle. Once visitors climb its steps to the upper level, they are rewarded with a majestic view of Fantasyland.

Playing cards stand guard before the Queen's castle at Disneyland.

Fashionable Alice

Between *Alice's Adventures in Wonderland* and *Through the Looking-Glass*, Alice undergoes a subtle fashion change. Although her dress remains largely the same, Tenniel gives her striped horizontal stockings and a headband in the second book. Both of these newly fashionable accessories marked Alice as a contemporary girl of her time. In turn, Tenniel's illustrations made headbands even more fashionable, and they became known as Alice bands.

Through the years and into our current century, Alice continues to make her mark on the fashions and styles of the day. Designers as different as Donatella Versace, Stella McCartney, Jason Wu, and Antonio Marras have been inspired by *Alice in Wonderland*. And in 2010, OPI launched a nail polish collection to tie in with the release of Tim Burton's *Alice in Wonderland*. Shades included "Off with Her Red," "Mad as a Hatter," and "Absolutely Alice."

Above and right: Models for designer Yasutaka Funakoshi strut their stuff at the "Alice in Wonderland in Me" fashion show in Tokyo in 2012.

Vogue Magazine
(December 2003)

When Grace Coddington, *Vogue*'s creative director, teamed up with the photographer Annie Leibovitz in 2003, the pair produced one of the magazine's most-talked-about fashion shoots. Based on *Alice's Adventures in Wonderland* and *Through the Looking-Glass*, the feature starred the Russian model Natalia Vodianova decked out as Alice in a series of blue frocks made especially for her. Leibovitz then shot Vodianova against a backdrop of fantastical sets, each inspired by Tenniel's illustrations. Cast as characters from the books were iconic fashion designers, including Christian LaCroix (the March Hare), Tom Ford (the White Rabbit), Marc Jacobs (the Caterpillar), and Stephen Jones (the Hatter). The success of the feature led to other storybook issues, like *The Wizard of Oz* in 2005.

Printemps Window Display
(December 2010)

In 2009, the Parisian department store Printemps invited a handful of top fashion designers to create one-of-a-kind dresses for its Alice-themed window display. Couture designers Alexander McQueen, Christopher Kane, Chloé, and Ann Demeulemeester, among others, obliged, and in March of the following year, the window display was revealed, just in time to correspond with the release of Tim Burton's *Alice in Wonderland*. Using black-and-white stills from the film as backdrops, mannequins with the heads of white rabbits were posed next to oversized teacups, playing cards, a pocket watch, and other Wonderland props. Two other department stores—New York's Bloomingdale's and London's Selfridges—also celebrated the Disney movie by designing Wonderland displays for their windows.

ALEXANDER MCQUEEN
1969 – 2010. Artiste

Sadly, Alexander McQueen wasn't able to see his creation. The noted designer had committed suicide a month earlier.

Tattooed Alice

According to an informal poll by *PWxyz*, a news blog of *Publishers Weekly*, *Alice's Adventures in Wonderland* rates second in the Top 5 Books That Inspire the Most Tattoos. It is also distinguished as inspiring the most varied collection of tattoos of any book. With its wide range of eccentric characters and quotations, an Alice devotee has a host of options to choose from. The most often inked quotation is the Cheshire Cat's "We're all mad here." So what book came in at number one? Kurt Vonnegut's *Slaughterhouse-Five* with its "So it goes" tattooed on the wrists, backs, shins, and feet of its many fans.

It took Holly Azzara almost a year to tattoo the entire story of Disney's *Alice in Wonderland* on the back, shoulders, and arms of Lake Jurosko.

Bejeweled Alice

Approached by Disney and asked to create some pieces to help promote Tim Burton's upcoming *Alice in Wonderland*, jeweler Tom Binns launched a line of Alice-inspired jewelry in 2010. Binns, who has designed pieces for people as disparate as Michelle Obama and Lady Gaga, let his punk sensibility run free and crafted bracelets, necklaces, and rings for his collaboration with Disney. Six limited-edition pieces each featured a specific Wonderland character or episode, including the Cheshire Cat, the Hatter, and the Mad Tea Party. Binns' favorite character, the Red Queen, was represented by a necklace in which, Binns said, he "interspersed red lacquered hearts with vicious little pins and thorns." The collection was priced at $1,000 to $1,500. A lower-priced collection of forty pieces was designed as well.

Steampunk Alice

Ann and Jeff VanderMeer, editors of the anthology *Steampunk*, identify their subject matter as "dark pseudo-Victorian fun." That definition certainly fits the bill when it comes to Carroll's Alice books. The term "steampunk" originally applied to a genre of science fiction that featured steam-powered technology in the Victorian era. Gradually, the steampunk movement expanded to include other categories such as film, video games, and fashion. In his novel *Automated Alice* (see page 133), Jeff Noon used elements of steampunk when he created the titular character as a robot. Tim Burton's *Alice in Wonderland* film relies heavily on steampunk imagery, and American McGee's dark video game that bears his name (see page 166) features an array of steampunk machines.

But perhaps the Alice books' effect on steampunk can best be seen in fashion. The dapper White Rabbit's vest and pocket watch have appeared as accessories for both men and women, while the Hatter's top hat has been reinterpreted in many styles. For women, Alice's striped tights and a corseted version of her blue dress have jazzed up many a steampunk closet. A few adventurous brides and grooms have even chosen an *Alice in Wonderland* theme for their weddings, donning Victorian finery and choosing Wonderland-themed décor and favors.

Psychedelic Alice

In the 1960s, *Alice's Adventures in Wonderland* was adopted by the counterculture as a kind of mascot for recreational drug use. Jefferson Airplane's hit "White Rabbit" (see page 149) strengthened the connection between Alice's ingesting of a mushroom and subsequent size changes, which were interpreted as hallucinations. Other references to drugs include the "Eat Me" cake that Alice consumes and the hookah-smoking Caterpillar.

The association between *Alice's Adventures in Wonderland* and drugs continues into the present day with a surprisingly large number of people believing that Lewis Carroll took hallucinogenic drugs while writing his books. Search for "Alice in Wonderland" and "drugs" on the Internet, and close to two million hits will appear. In fact, it is highly unlikely that Carroll ever indulged. For one thing, LSD wasn't synthesized until 1938, forty years after Carroll's death. And while opium was popular in Victorian times, there is no evidence whatsoever to support Carroll ever ingesting it.

At one time, this ubiquitous poster could be found in nearly every student dorm room.

Curious Alice

(1968)

An educational film aimed at eight- to ten-year-olds, *Curious Alice* is a short filmstrip with an anti-drug message. Funded by the National Institute for Mental Health, it purports to warn children about the dangers of experimenting with mind-altering substances. The film starts with Alice falling asleep over a book and landing in a room full of drug paraphernalia. From there, she goes on to meet many of the characters from Wonderland who are now strung out on various drugs. The Caterpillar smokes marijuana from his hookah and the King of Hearts keeps the other cards in line by doping them with heroin. The Mad Tea Party has turned into a Mad Drug Party with the Hatter tripping on LSD, a twitchy March Hare jumping about on amphetamines, and a sleepy Dormouse stoned on barbiturates. Throughout her dream, Alice resists the temptations pushed on her and sternly lectures the drug users on the dangers of their habits.

Despite its efforts to warn children away from drugs, the filmstrip almost appears to do the opposite. For starters, there is an obvious contradiction that undermines the message. Soon after arriving in Wonderland, Alice sees and picks up the "Drink Me" bottle—a vessel containing an unknown substance—and drains it. She then exclaims, "Oh! Oh, wow!" To the viewer, it strongly appears as if Alice took some type of mind-altering drug and is now under its effects. Furthering this interpretation is the psychedelic, trippy animation that makes drugs look like fun. In 1972, the National Coordinating Council on Drug Education criticized *Curious Alice* as being counterproductive, stating that children "may be intrigued by the fantasy world of drugs" after viewing it.

Alice in Wonderland Syndrome

Imagine suddenly feeling like your whole body is growing, glancing at your hands and seeing your fingers to what looks to be a mile or so away. Or perhaps you feel yourself shrinking, becoming smaller and smaller until everyday objects loom above you. For people who suffer from Alice in Wonderland Syndrome (AIWS), these spatial disturbances can be a common occurrence. First identified in 1955 by John Todd, a British psychiatrist, the syndrome is named after Carroll's book and the little girl who throughout her adventures in Wonderland finds herself changing size again and again.

Associated with migraine headaches, the syndrome typically afflicts young children, its symptoms becoming more severe as they enter the teen years. Many children grow out of it entirely; in others, the episodes fade or the gaps between them grow longer. The symptoms, which can range from mild to severe, can include visual distortions of one's body, as described above, or visual distortions of objects. In the latter, a person might experience an approaching car to be the size of an Army tank and have difficulty judging its distance, making crossing the street a dangerous undertaking. Some people experience problems with their balance or the way in which they perceive texture. One sufferer felt as if what he knew to be straight floors curved or dipped as he walked on them. There is no known cure for AIWS, so sufferers must learn how to manage their lives to reduce symptoms. Interestingly, Lewis Carroll was known to be afflicted with migraines, and some critics have speculated that the author of *Alice's Adventures in Wonderland* may have experienced visual distortions and thereby gotten some of his ideas for Alice's bodily transformations while under their influence.

The Alice Project

The brainchild of the late Randy Pausch, a professor at Carnegie Mellon University, *Alice* is free educational software that allows children to create 3-D animation programs. The software, which was released in 1999, teaches kids to program almost without them realizing that they are doing so. According to Pausch, "the best way to teach somebody something is to have them think they're learning something else." With *Alice*, children learn to program as they're making movies and video games. Pausch, who considered the *Alice* project his legacy, named the program after Carroll's Alice books in homage to the author and mathematician. "Lewis Carroll was one of the greatest mathematicians of his day," Pausch stated. "But he also knew how to make things incredibly simple. It's obvious that virtual reality is a good metaphor for stepping through the looking-glass."

Pausch died in 2008 at age forty-seven from pancreatic cancer, but not before seeing his baby launched. More than one million people have downloaded *Alice*, and several textbooks have been published about it. *Alice 3*, the latest beta version, was recently released, and features the animated characters from the PC game *The Sims 2*.

Alice in Japan

According to Sean Somers' essay in *Alice Beyond Wonderland*, "Japanese translators have paid more attention to Lewis Carroll than any other British author." Starting in the late nineteenth century, these translations were solely for children and were heavily abridged and revised to accommodate Japanese culture. Early illustrators, likewise, adapted Carroll's story to make it more palatable to Japanese taste. Alice had Japanese features and wore a kimono in the illustrations. By 2007, though, when Sakura Kinoshita's manga version of *Alice in Wonderland*

(*Fushigi No Kuni No Arisu*) was published, all that had changed. Her Alice has long blond hair and enormous, wide-open eyes, and she is dressed in her iconic blue dress and white pinafore.

Kinoshita's *Fushigi No Kuni No Arisu*.

The character of Alice has proved to be a popular choice for writers of manga, Japan's version of comics. Among the many adaptations of Alice and her romp through Wonderland are Clamp's *Fushigi no Kuni no Miyuki-chan* (*Miyuki-chan in Wonderland*), which offers a humorous lesbian take on the story, and Jun Mochizuki's *Pandora Hātsu* (*Pandora Hearts*), which has numerous references to the Alice books and features Oz, a fifteen-year-old boy based on the White Rabbit and with whom a girl named Alice is in love with.

Quin Rose's *Hāto no Kuni no Arisu* (*Alice in the Country of Hearts*) is the most well known of the manga works. The books originally started as a video game and were followed by a series of manga, novels, and an anime film. This Alice is taken against her will by Peter White, a grown man with floppy bunny ears, and brought to Wonderland, a strange place divided into countries, one of which is the Heartland of the title. Peter is in love with Alice, and soon the rest of Heartland's inhabitants become smitten with her as well. Heartland, though, is undergoing a civil war with the three territories fighting each other for control. Familiar Wonderland characters appear, although they are all in human form. There's Vivaldi (the Queen of Hearts), who rules the Castle of Hearts; Blood Dupre (the Hatter), who oversees the Hatters, a Mafialike group from Hatter Mansion; and Boris Airay (the Cheshire Cat), who lives in the Amusement Park. Created with young girls in mind, *Alice in the Country of Hearts* features a lot of romantic intrigue between Alice and the young men vying for her attention.

Hello Kitty's Alice in Wonderland (1993)

With her trademark red bow and lack of a visible mouth, Hello Kitty is a multi-billion-dollar brand. Created in 1974 by the Japanese company Sanrio, the expressionless white feline's official name is Kitty White and she lives in London with her family. Despite her Japanese origins, Hello Kitty is firmly British, largely because many Japanese girls were Anglophiles at the time she was created. Kitty's name took its inspiration from one of Dinah's kittens in *Through the Looking-Glass*. (To confuse the matter, the black kitten was called Kitty while the white one was Snowdrop.) Fittingly, Hello Kitty went on to star in an animated version of *Alice in Wonderland* in 1993. Released on home video in Japan and airing on CBS in the United States, the episode featured Hello Kitty in the role of Alice. Just over thirty minutes in length, the didactic plot is faithful to Carroll's original, although unlike Alice, Hello Kitty is eager to find her way home.

Below: A lively window display at Fortnum & Mason in London featuring the Mad Hatter's Tea Party.

Alice in Wonderland Restaurants

Theme restaurants are popular in Japan. In Tokyo alone there are eateries that are dedicated to ninjas, vampires, and even Alcatraz's infamous prison. It shouldn't come as a surprise, then, to learn that there are at least four Alice-themed restaurants in the country. All were designed by Fantastic Design Works and are located throughout Japan. The most recent is Tokyo's Alice in Magic World. The family-friendly restaurant is divided into separate dining areas, such as the Magic Forest and the Mad Tea Party room. Waitresses dressed in Alice costumes greet you and take your orders. Appetizers are served on a chessboard and dishes come with "Eat Me" tags. Diners can choose from a varied menu, which include such dishes as Green Caterpillar Tuna and Mock Turtle Mimosa Salad.

Located in Tokyo, this Alice-themed restaurant features booths decorated to resemble a croquet lawn.

Fans of Alice

Fan Fiction

Fan fiction writers aren't in it for the money. Inspired by a favorite character—from a book, movie, TV show, or even a game—these fans write stories to supplement or continue where the original left off and publish their works online on sites created specifically for such a purpose. In the 1960s, fans of *Star Trek* were the first to popularize the form, penning fan fiction for mimeographed fanzines distributed at conventions. Today, millions of writers flock online to post their stories, which feature countless characters from pop culture. With its slogan "Unleash your imagination," Fanfiction.net is the premiere fan fiction site. Established in 1998, it boasts more than two million users.

Fans of *Alice's Adventures in Wonderland* who go to the site can find a wealth of stories to choose from. As of this writing, Fanfiction.net hosted close to three thousand works featuring *Alice's Adventures in Wonderland*, with stories written in English, Spanish, and French, among others. Some writers stick to Carroll's basic structure and tweak some of the episodes, such as including Alice's pet cat Dinah in her fall down the rabbit hole, or give it a new ending. Others change the story significantly, offering Gothic or romantic versions. A popular sub-genre is the crossover in which a writer weaves different characters from pop culture into a single story. In such cases, Alice might be paired with Peter Pan and the two might sail off to Neverland together. Or Harry Potter might find his way to Wonderland and share the caterpillar's hookah. There are even stories dedicated to furthering the adventures of Alice adaptations. Fans of the game *American McGee's Alice* write stories about her, as do fans of the Tim Burton movie.

Stories can range from a few paragraphs to a full-length novel with multiple characters and a twisty plot. As with any genre, works can vary greatly in quality. Many are not particularly well written, are riddled with spelling errors, and suffer from poor grammar. A few, though, rise above the rest and stand out for their engaging story lines and flair for language. Since readers can comment on the stories, competent fan writers can gather a following of their own, with reviewers clamoring for the next story installment.

Fan artist Jaume Vilanova illustrated this scene of Alice conversing with the Caterpillar.

Fan Art

Just as fans are inspired to write additional stories about the Alice books, they are also drawn to creating art about the characters. One of the major sites where budding artists post their works online is deviantART.com. Works can be as simple as a black-and-white sketch of the Cheshire Cat or as elaborate as a full-color scene of Alice escaping from the Queen of Hearts. Crossover exists in fan art too. One artist turned Alice into a mermaid and placed her in an underwater Wonderland that resembles Disney's *The Little Mermaid*.

Right and below: Zsófia Szabó, a fan artist from Hungary, created her illustrations from cut paper.

Far right: A collection of colorful illustrations—including a bored Alice at the Mad Hatter's tea party—by artist Jaume Vilanova.

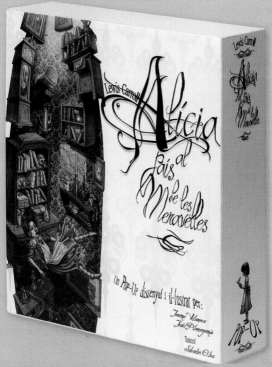

Above: Contemporary artist Jonathan Barry's piece entitled "Who Stole the Tarts?" is an oil on canvas painting.

Left: Some of the incredible animals of Wonderland are represented in this artwork by artist Lisbeth Zwerger.

The Lewis Carroll Societies

Founded in 1969, The Lewis Carroll Society (UK) is an organization dedicated to the life, works, and influence of the man who created the Alice books. The Society puts out three publications: *The Carrollian* (formerly *Jabberwocky*), a scholarly journal; *Bandersnatch*, a newsletter; and the *Lewis Carroll Review*. Three sister societies have been formed: The Lewis Carroll Society of North America (1974), which puts out a semiannual magazine, *Knight Letter*, and maintains a very active website, blog, and publications program; The Lewis Carroll Society of Japan (1994); and the Lewis Carroll Society of Brazil (2009).

Index

Sources and Further Reading

Lewis Carroll's Major Works

Alice's Adventures in Wonderland. 1865.
Phantasmagoria. 1869.
Through the Looking-Glass, and What Alice Found There. 1871.
The Hunting of the Snark. 1876.
Rhyme? And Reason? 1883.
A Tangled Tale. 1885.
Alice's Adventures under Ground. 1886.
Sylvie and Bruno. 1889.
The Nursery "Alice." 1889.
Sylvie and Bruno Concluded. 1893.

Biographies

Lewis Carroll

Cohen, Morton N. *Lewis Carroll: A Biography.* (Macmillan, London: 1995).
Leach, Karoline. *In the Shadow of the Dreamchild: A New Understanding of Lewis Carroll.* (Peter Owen, London: 1999).
Woolf, Jenny. *The Mystery of Lewis Carroll: Discovering the Whimsical, Thoughtful, and Sometimes Lonely Man Who Created "Alice in Wonderland."* (St. Martin's Press, New York: 2010).

Alice Liddell

Amor, Anne Clark. *The Real Alice.* (Michael Joseph, London: 1981).

John Tenniel

Morris, Frankie. *Artist of Wonderland: The Life, Political Cartoons, and Illustrations of Tenniel.* (University of Virginia, Charlottesville: 2005).

Commentary

Brookner, Will. *Alice's Adventures: Lewis Carroll in Popular Culture.* (Bloomsbury Academic, London: 2005).
Davies, Mark J. *Alice in Waterland: Lewis Carroll and the River Thames in Oxford.* (Signal Books, Oxford: 2010).
Gardner, Martin. *The Annotated Alice: The Definitive Edition.* (W.W. Norton, New York: 1999).
Hollingsworth, Christopher (Editor). *Alice Beyond Wonderland: Essays for the Twenty-First Century.* (University of Iowa Press, Iowa City: 2009).
Ovenden, Graham (Editor). *The Illustrators of Alice in Wonderland.* (St. Martin's Press, New York: 1972).
Sigler, Carolyn (Editor). *Alternative Alices: Visions and Revisions of Lewis Carroll's Alice Books.* (The University Press of Kentucky, Lexington: 1997).
Steffel, Stephanie Lovett. *The Art of Alice in Wonderland.* (Smithmark, New York: 1998).
Yoe, Craig. *Alice in Comicland.* (IDW Publishing, San Diego: 2014).

Picture Credits

Back cover: *The Queen has come!*
Illustration by Sir John Tenniel 1871
© Walker Art Library / Alamy

Introduction

p.ii and throughout: © Shutterstock

p.iii: *Cheshire Cat* © Ken Turner
(Beehive Illustration)

p.iv: © Shutterstock

p.iv and throughout: old paper texture
© Shutterstock

p.v: *Alice in Wonderland* by Philip
Mendoza © Look and Learn /
Bridgeman Images

p.vi: © Lisbeth Zwerger

p.ix: *Alice* © Ken Turner (Beehive
Illustration)

p.x: *The White Rabbit*, 2003, Broomfield,
Frances © Frances Broomfield / Portal
Gallery, London / Bridgeman Images

p.xiii: *In the Duchess's Kitchen* by Arthur
Rackham (1867–1939) © Private
Collection / Bridgeman Images

Chapter 1

p.xiv: *Alice and the Dodo*. Illustration by
Sir John Tenniel 1871 © Walker Art
Library / Alamy

p.1 and throughout: Vintage label ©
Shutterstock

p.1: Alice cover 1908 © Mary Evans
Picture Library / Alamy

p.2: Edith, Ina and Alice Liddell on
sofa, 1858. Photograph by Lewis
Carroll © SSPL via Getty Images

pp.3–4: © The British Library / The
Image Works

p.5: *Alice and the Dodo*. Illustration by
Sir John Tenniel 1871 © Walker Art
Library / Alamy

p.6: © British Library / Robana / R /
Rex USA

p.7: © Mary Evans Picture Library / Alamy

p.8: © The British Library / The Image
Works

p.9: © SSPL via Getty Images

p.11: © Getty images

p.12: *The White Rabbit* by John
Tenniel,(1820–1914) © Private
Collection / Bridgeman Images

p.13 left: © Pictorial Press Ltd / Alamy

p.13 right: *The Dormouse in the Teapot*
by John Tenniel (1820–1914) (after)
Private Collection / © Look and
Learn / Bridgeman Images

p.14 left: *Alice in the Sheep's Shop* by Sir
John Tenniel © Timewatch Images /
Alamy

p.14 right: By John Tenniel (1820–1914)
© AF Fotografie / Alamy

p.15: *The Queen has come!* Illustration by
Sir John Tenniel 1871 © Walker Art
Library / Alamy

pp.16–17: © Getty images

Chapter 2

p.18: © Lisbeth Zwerger

p.19: *Mad Hatter* by Philip Mendoza ©
Look and Learn / Bridgeman Images

p.20 left: © The LIFE Picture
Collection / Getty Images

p.20 right: © Heritage Images / Getty
Images

p.21: *The Duchess with her Family* by John
Tenniel © Classic Image / Alamy

p.22 left: *Knight, Death and the Devil*,
1513 by Albrecht Dürer (1471–1528) ©
Hungarian National Gallery, Budapest,
Hungary / Bridgeman Images

p.22 right: © Timewatch Images / Alamy

p.23: © Peter Newell

pp.24 and 25 top right. © Stapleton
Collection / Corbis

p.25 bottom left: *The White Rabbit* by
Arthur Rackham (1867–1939) © Peter
Nahum at The Leicester Galleries,
London / Bridgeman Images

p.26: Willy Pogany (Hungarian-
American, 1882–1955) *Alice's
Flamingo, Alice's Adventures in
Wonderland* page 124. Image supplied
by Meier And Sons Rare Books

p.27: Reprinted by permission of
Peters Fraser & Dunlop (www.
petersfraserdunlop.com) on behalf
of Mervyn Peake

p.28 left: © Salvador Dalí, Fundació
Gala-Salvador Dalí, Artists Rights
Society (ARS), New York 2014.
Courtesy Stapleton Collection / Corbis

p.28 right: Max Ernst. © 2014 Artists
Rights Society (ARS), New York /
ADAGP, Paris

p.29: © Ralph Steadman.

pp.30–31: © Barry Moser

pp.32–33: Illustration © 1999
Helen Oxenbury. From
*ALICE'S ADVENTURES IN
WONDERLAND* illustrated by
Helen Oxenbury Reproduced by
permission of Walker Books Ltd,
London SE11 5HJ www.walker.co.uk

p.34 left: Mabel Lucie Attwell Courtesy

pp.137–137: TM and © DC Comics

p.138: Bongo Comics: Reprinted from *Lisa Comics #1: Lisa in Wordland.* © 1995 Bongo Entertainment, Inc. The Simpsons TM & © Twentieth Century Fox Film Corporation. All Rights Reserved.

p.139: *The Alice in Wonderland Cookbook*, 1976. All reasonable attempts have been made to contact the copyright holders of all images. You are invited to contact the publisher if your image was used without identification or acknowledgment.

p.140 background: © Shutterstock

p.140: Reprinted with the permission of Little Simon, an imprint of Simon & Schuster Children's Publishing Division from *ALICE'S ADVENTURES IN WONDERLAND* (Pop-Up Adaptation) by Robert Sabuda. Copyright © 2003 Robert Sabuda.

p.141: Babylit colour primer © Alison Oliver – artist / Jennifer Adams – author / Gibbs Smith Publisher

pp.142–144: Reprinted with the permission of Little Simon, an imprint of Simon & Schuster Children's Publishing Division from *ALICE'S ADVENTURES IN WONDERLAND* (Pop-Up Adaptation) by Robert Sabuda. Copyright © 2003 Robert Sabuda.

p.145 top left: © British Library / Robana via Getty Images

p.145 top middle: © British Library / Robana / R / Rex USA

p.145 center left: © Mary Evans Picture Library / Alamy

p.145 center middle: © Lebrecht Authors/ Lebrecht Music & Arts/Corbis

p.145 bottom right: Courtesy The Little Book Store at www.thelittlebookstore.co.uk

p.146: © Getty Images

p.148: © FromOldBooks.org / Alamy

p.149 far right: © Shutterstock

p.149 right: *The Mad Hatter* / Chick Corea © Polydor

p.150 left: *Goodbye Alice in Wonderland* / Jewel © Atlantic Records

p.150 right: *Alice* / Tom Waits © Epitaph Records

p.150 bottom: © Shutterstock

p.151: © Redferns / Getty Images

p.152: © The LIFE Images Collection / Getty Images

p.153: *Alice in Wonderland*, Mendoza, Philip (1898–1973) © Look and Learn / Bridgeman Images

p.153 background: © Shutterstock

Chapter 8

p.154: *Alice in Wonderland*, Mendoza, Philip (1898-1973) © Look and Learn / Bridgeman Images

p.155 left: Toys: Photograph by Stewart Mark, Camera Press London.

p.155 right: Cards: © Shutterstock

pp.157–158: © Victoria and Albert Museum, London

p.159 left: De La Rue box. All reasonable attempts have been made to contact the copyright holders of all images. You are invited to contact the publisher if your image was used without identification or acknowledgment.

p.159 right: The Mad Hatter Carreras Cigarette Card. c.1929 © Lake County Discovery Museum / UIG / Bridgeman Images

p.160: *The Queen of Hearts*, 1999 (oil on canvas), Barry, Jonathan © Private Collection / Bridgeman Images

p.161 left: © Shutterstock

p.162: Original Sir John Tenniel hand painted chessboard. Images courtesy of the brand *Alice Through the Looking Glass* ®

p.162 background: © Shutterstock

p.163: © Yasmin Sethi

p.164: © Shutterstock

p.167 top: *American McGee's Alice* image used with permission of Electronic Arts Inc.

p.167 bottom: © Zsófia Szabó – Graphic designer and Illustrator www.behance.net/ZsofiaSzabo and www.ZsofiaSzabo.tumblr.com

pp.168–169: © Atomic Antelope

pp170–171: © Guinness images courtesy of Diageo Ireland

p.172 top left: Doll by © "Katy and the cat" www.artworks-snezana.blogspot.it

p.172 top right and bottom: © Courtesy of The Strong®, Rochester, New York

p.173: © Victoria and Albert Museum, London

p.174: dolls all © Courtesy of The Strong®, Rochester, New York

p.175: © Laperruque / Alamy

Chapter 9

p.176: © Sito Alvina (photographer). model: Andi Autumn

p.177: © Shutterstock

p.178: © SJH Photography / Alamy

p.179: © John Gaffen / Alamy

pp.180–181: © KIM KYUNG-HOON / Reuters / Corbis

p.182: © Marzari Emanuele / Sipa

p.183: © WENN UK / Alamy

p.184: © Alexandria LaNier

p.185: © Sito Alvina (photographer). model: Andi Autumn

p.185 right: © Shutterstock

p.186: All reasonable attempts have been made to contact the copyright holders of all images. You are invited to contact the publisher if your image was used without identification or acknowledgment.

p.186 background: © Shutterstock

p.188: © 2006 Sakura Kinoshita, GENTOSHA COMICS INC. Japan

p.189: Photograph by Richard Stonehouse, Camera Press London

p.190: © WENN UK / Alamy

pp.191 & 193: © Jaume Vilanova i Bartrolí (Illustrator and paper engineer) www.jaumevilanova.com / Jesús Planagumà i Valls (Graphic designer)

p.192: © Zsófia Szabó – Graphic designer and Illustrator www.behance.net/ZsofiaSzabo and www.ZsofiaSzabo.tumblr.com

p.194: © Lisbeth Zwerger

p.195: *Who Stole the Tarts?* 2000 (oil on canvas), Barry, Jonathan © Private Collection / Bridgeman Images